SAILING
To Your
SUCCESS

Keys to Your Personal and Professional Development

Dedication

To Theresa
who through her unique sense of humor
not only has
kept me supplied with funny stories to share
in my writing and speaking
but even more
has demonstrated to me
the depth and meaning of true friendship

SAILING
To Your
SUCCESS

Keys to Your Personal and Professional Development

by **MARGE KNOTH**

Copyright © 1999 by Marge Knoth
ALL RIGHTS RESERVED
No part of this book may be reproduced
in any form or by any electronic means
without written permission from the author.

ISBN: 0-927935-12-0
First Edition, March, 1999

Table of Contents

CHAPTER		PAGE
1	Being Freely Yourself--and Loving It	7
2	Growing Into Who You Really Are	17
3	Recognizing and Developing Your Unique Gifts	27
4	Leadership Struggles: Leadership Solutions	35
5	The Benefit of Failure	45
6	Attitude Begins With You	53
7	Polishing Your People-Pleasing Powers	62
8	Patiently Prevailing Over Procrastination	70
9	The Power of the Spoken Word	81
10	The Gift of Listening	91
11	Your Body Has a Language of Its Own	99
12	Goals are Dreams in Disguise	110

13	Making Time Count	119
14	Points To Ponder on the Path To Professionalism	123
15	Coping With Criticism Constructively	133
16	Clutter, Confusion, and Chaos	141
17	Friendship: A Present You Give Yourself	150
18	Caution: Giving Generously Can Be Habit-Forming	159
19	Finding Success in Your Profession	167
**	Other Books by the Author	173

CHAPTER 1

Being Freely Yourself-- And Loving It

The judgments we make about ourselves are some of the most important we will ever make. How we view ourselves, whether on the job, or in life as a whole, can make an unbelievable difference in our overall happiness and contentment.

How do *you* see yourself--highly successful, outgoing, likable, accepted? Or is it more like inferior, tolerated, disliked, unattractive, unpopular? Who set the standards of how you think of yourself, of your worth? Was it your parents, teachers, other kids, the neighborhood where your grew up?

Think back, way back to childhood. Remember those games on the school playground where teams were chosen, where the players were selected one by one? Remember waiting, even praying: "God, don't let me be last." If you were regularly selected first, no doubt your self-esteem was flying high even then. *I am liked. I must be an okay person. I feel good about myself.* More than likely you grew up and are still feeling good about yourself.

But if you were the *last* chosen, or nearly the last, how did you feel? *They don't like me. I must not be any good. I'd better not get too involved in their games. I don't want them to reject me again.* Did that one little episode, incorrectly recorded in your tender young mind, have a part in forming a negative opinion of yourself? Have you considered that that one untrue childlike assumption may still be directing your feelings and actions as an adult today? Those muted, jumbled, unclear feelings can all be summed up in a word-- *self-esteem.*

What is self-esteem anyway? Self-esteem is how we see ourselves. Webster's dictionary defines *esteem* as "to value highly, respect, to consider, favorable opinion." The Webster's Thesaurus gives these words as synonyms for *esteem:* honor, admiration, respect, revere, cherish, treasure, regard. Do we not use these words, though, to describe *others?* Surely not ourselves!

Each one of us is a unique and valued creation; there is no one else in all the world just like us. Yet how often do we go about believing lies from childhood? "We are not this." or "We are not that." or "We are not like someone else." Consequently, there must be something "wrong" with us. So we don our masks and imitate another person or persons who we think are "right." Thus we hide from the world the unique person we really are.

Positive self-esteem is a basic human need. We all need to be accepted, liked, cared about. In the confines of your facility or business, which is a little world in itself, it's especially important. If we think we don't measure up to our superior's or even our peers standards for us, we are probably feeling badly about ourselves and our self-esteem is suffering.

Positive self-esteem energizes and motivates us. It allows us to function better in our companies, to take our bumps and pull ourselves right back up. People with high self-esteem accomplish more, are happier, and have a positive influence on the people they work and live with. Dr. Wolf J. Rinke in his article "How to Develop a Positive Attitude, How to Maintain a Positive Attitude" in *Bottom Line Personal* writes, " When you think positively about yourself, you work harder at what you want to do--and give up less easily. You make a better impression on others, which encourages them to help you. When you think more positively about your colleagues, employees, spouse, and children, you build stronger and more productive relationships--leading to greater success at work and at home."

Low self-esteem, on the other hand, causes people to feel hopeless, depressed, and lethargic. It drains energy and makes them less productive. When we see people who escape to drugs, alcohol, promiscuity, and anger toward others, we will probably discover that they are people with very low self-esteem. One Gallup poll found that on the average, 37% of Americans have high self-esteem, 33% average, and 30% low. Those polled who were suffering from low self-esteem were focused on achieving, getting ahead at work, and obtaining material possessions. On the other hand, those with high self-esteem were centered more on keeping a clear mind, and having good family relationships. To them, success meant happiness, not things.

How does one get self-esteem? Psychologist Oriville Urim did a study and found two main sources for self-esteem: mastery of one's environment, and a feeling of being positively valued by others. Mastery is associated with having a sense of power and control in some area of our life--perhaps our career or our social world. Being valued comes from intimate relationships with friends, family, even some coworkers. There needs to be a balance between mastery and being valued.

Words have a profound effect on how we view ourselves. Perhaps our parents unwittingly planted negative thought patterns in us by attacking our person rather than our behavior: "You are a bad girl!" not "That was a bad thing you did." Maybe it was school kids, neighbor kids, or teachers. Used wrongly, words can batter our self-image and lower our self-esteem. Words can attack our person as a whole, or any small segment of how we view ourselves.

For instance, when I was in 4th grade the music teacher said, "Someone in the back is flat." She listened a little longer and then she pointed me out--in front of the whole class!

"You! Just move your lips," she said, "but don't let any sounds come out."

For a sensitive nine-year-old, that was a blow. Until my thirties, I was so self-conscious about my singing ability that I didn't even let my husband hear me sing. Then I was led to join our large church choir and they received me with open arms. Still, singing is not my gift, but I'm mature enough now to know I can't have all the gifts. I will use my stronger ones and let others strong in my weak areas pick up the slack. Our self-esteem is lowered when we believe lies about ourselves. Sure I was flat that day, but it did not necessarily mean I was a hopeless case. Yet my childish mind made that association. *I am really a bad singer.* The lie was planted and took root. And I grew up believing it. In reality, a little voice-training may have been all that I needed.

We all respond differently to negativity in our lives which can affect our self-esteem. Many are knocked off balance by it; others use negativity in a positive way. My Scottish friend, Theresa, should know what low self-esteem is all about.

At three, she was left an orphan in Scotland when her mother died. Theresa went to live with an aunt. At seven she was hospitalized for five months with rheumatic fever. Three times a week visitors were allowed in the ward. "Three times a week," she remembers, "I would watch that door open, and hope. I would see everyone else getting visitors, but I was always disappointed. No one came to see me for months and months. I know about self-esteem."

Then when she was finally able to return to school, she was strapped and bruised across the knuckles because she could not catch up and learn--in just a few days--all the mathematic tables the other kids had learned over the five months of her illness. But Theresa, rather than believing the lies that she was no good or dumb, toughened up and learned to fend for herself. She developed a sense of humor and learned to laugh at unpleasant situations in life. Today, unusually compassionate of heart, she boldly stands up and speaks out, unafraid, when people are being hurt or treated unfairly. Her self-image could have been destroyed, but it wasn't.

As Eleanor Roosevelt once said, "Nobody can make you feel inferior without your permission."

The average person generates 60,000 thoughts a day. Ninety-five percent of them follow the same association paths. Experts say that we need to cut new grooves in our thinking. In other words, get out of the rut, think and do things differently. Don't continue thinking and acting wrongly just because "that's the way we grew up thinking and doing." Even those with high self-esteem sometimes struggle with incorrect negative impressions about themselves.

Again, self-esteem is how we see ourselves. We must grab hold of those 60,000 thoughts and re-channel the negative ones. We need to make new thought patterns, positive ones. Treat ourselves as a friend, not an enemy. We need to give ourselves positive self talk. "I am an intelligent person. I may have made some mistakes in that project, but look at all the good ones I have completed in the past." or "Well, I *did* eat that hot fudge sundae. And I enjoyed it! Sure it was a lot of calories, but I will watch my intake the next few days." Walt

Kelly once said "We have met the enemy and he is us."
We can blame others, blame our circumstance, but when it comes down to it, low self-esteem is often there because our thinking is wrong.

So how do we go about learning to think more healthy thoughts about ourselves when our feelings may be screaming to the contrary. Louisa Rogers in her article "Nurturing Yourself with Self-Esteem" published in *Care Notes* says, "Often we try to hide our real feelings with food or drink or activity. Begin to feel, face them. When we allow ourselves to experience our feelings, we realize that feelings are only feelings. They lose their pull. It's the suppression and censoring of feelings that gives them power."

You might ask, "Is there anything else I can do to keep my self-esteem high?" Yes, there are many things. First, as much as you can control, eliminate people from your life who make you feel put down or inferior. Replace them with positive people, people who make you feel good about yourself, who may know your shortcomings but like you anyway.

Praise yourself and compliment yourself as well as others. This builds positive self-esteem. There are always foes out there anxious to criticize you. I've said it before, "Don't join them." You are okay just as you are. Befriend yourself. Do something nice for yourself every day. Allow yourself a few minutes to prop your feet up and enjoy a cup of tea and a good book. Make a list of things that bring you pleasure-- chewing gum, walking in the moonlight, shopping, talking on the phone, flipping through a magazine, or working out at a fitness center. I'm not advocating narcissism. I'm simply saying to treat yourself as you would a good friend.

As Geneen Roth says in *Breaking Free From Compulsive Eating,* "When you befriend yourself, you discover that there's somebody home, and when you've been knocking at the door for years without getting an answer, that's very reassuring."

Savor and dwell on your successes. No *I'm* not a singer! But since childhood I wanted to be a writer. I began writing for magazines and was first published nationally in 1974. What a thrill! And I thought, "If I did it once, I surely could do it again." I said to myself, "Someday maybe I'll even write a book!" Thanks to the Good Lord, that dream has been fulfilled many times over. I will dwell on my accomplishments, not my weaknesses.

Someone once said, "Achievement will never rise higher than confidence." Expect to succeed. But be patient with yourself. Rome wasn't built in a day. Eddie Cantor aptly summed it up when he said, "It takes twenty years to make an overnight success."

Greet people with a smile. On introductions extend your hand and offer your first name. This speaks volumes about your self-confidence. When you make a phone call, give your name up-front to the person who answers--even before you state your business. Starting off with your name establishes that someone of importance is making the call.

How we accept compliments reveals a measure of our self-perception. How often when someone compliments our outfit do we say, "Oh this old thing?" or "Let me tell you about the bargain I got on it." If we're complimented for doing something nice for someone, do we come back with, "It was nothing." We should not deflect compliments, but rather gracefully accept them without putting ourselves down. Just kindly say, "Thank you."

Many of us become too security-minded. Self-esteem rises when we step out and take some risks. After all, "You can't steal second base and keep one foot on first."

Forgive yourself. Sure we've all done or said things we wish we hadn't, but it's time to make peace with ourself. Like heavy bags of groceries, unforgiveness is a grievous load to carry. And this weight pulls our self-esteem down, down, down. Consciously decide to forgive yourself for any mistakes or things you wish you had done differently. This may have to be a daily occurrence. *Choose* to forgive, and do it. Forgiveness is a tangible thing. It must be received, even from ourself to ourself. If I were to offer you a $100 bill, it would remain mine until you came and took it from my hand. In the same way, reach out and *receive* that forgiveness from yourself. One way is to write yourself a letter granting that forgiveness, and mail it to yourself. Then read it and receive your forgiveness.

We can't achieve any real success in life without a healthy self-esteem. Denis Waitley in his wonderful book *10 Secrets of Greatness* says, "Self acceptance, as we are right now, is the key to healthy self-esteem. Seeing ourselves as worthwhile, changing, imperfect, growing individuals, and knowing that although we are not born with equal mental and physical uniforms, we are born with the equal right to feel deserving of excellence according to our own spiritual standards. You are a masterpiece of creation. Always carry with you the secret: Love must be within us before it can be given."

And when we truly love ourselves, our self-esteem is high. Subsequently, that love will flow out from us to those in our care, and to those with whom we work and live each day. So open up your heart and become your own best friend.

CHAPTER 2

Growing Into Who You Really Are

Have you ever seen one of those basset hounds, as a pup, with its loose skin hanging on it like a size 24 dress on a size-six lady? Do you ever feel like that, wondering if you'll eventually grow into the person you really want to be? Do you get frustrated with yourself that you are not more tolerant, more bold, or perhaps less vocal? Well, if so, rest assured you are not alone. Most everyone strives to be a better person than they are.

Professionals are a unique breed of people. They are often giving, loving, and unselfish. But, if that is the case, you might ask, why are we so hard on ourselves? That's easy to answer. We *are people of character.*

So what is character? Someone once described it this way: "Character is what you are in the dark." In other words, we are only who we are when we are all alone. I got checked on this very issue the other day. I like to think of myself as a person of character. Unfortunately, I fall short far too often.

I was out running errands and thinking out this chapter on character while I was driving. I was in a hurry, as usual, traveling down a narrow country road with hardly another car in sight. The speed limit was what I considered an unreasonable 30 miles-per-hour. I glanced at my speedometer --almost 50. I knew there was not a policemen in sight. I was safe. Then the thought came to me: "Character is what you are in the dark." I realized I was being untruthful, and I was not allowing the virtue of patience to be developed within me. I touched the brake and determined to do better in the future.

Character is described in other ways, too. Helen Gahagan Douglas says, "Character isn't inherited. One builds it daily by the way one thinks and acts, thought by thought, action by action. If one lets fear or hate or anger take possession of the mind, they become self-forged chains."

Felix Frankfurter says, "Old age and sickness bring out the essential characteristics of a man." And isn't that true? How do we respond when we are tired, sick, criticized, corrected, or thrust into a frustrating or fearful situation? Do we get irritable and complain? Do we become defensive and self-righteous? Or do we smile and roll with the punches? Most of us would probably have to admit there's room in us for some character growth.

Character-building is different from self-improvement. I've always been big on self-improvement--studying to be a better writer, speaker, have a healthier body, manage my time better, become better organized. Self-improvement measures are helpful, sure, but they are generally short-term fixes. After a while, those things we have learned dim in our memory. Character, on the other hand, lasts a lifetime. Someone once said it's like the difference between owning a brand new economy car and big luxury car. The economy car with all the gee-gaws (self-improvement programs) may look great on the show room floor, but will it last? Will the paint hold up? Will it rust quickly? Will it still be purring at 200,000 miles? Or will it have served its purpose and now be resting in peace in an auto junk yard while the luxury car (character) is still doing its thing?

We deal with many people each day. We are visible in our company. We want to be the best we can be. We love people, care about them, and want to treat them well. We want a quality character within us to be apparent to all those with whom we deal. But sometimes, with all the frustrations of our jobs, we fall short. That is normal. Be patient with yourself. Character isn't formed overnight.

Helen Keller once said: "Character cannot be developed in ease and quiet. Only through experience of trial and suffering can the soul be strengthened, vision cleared, ambition inspired, and success achieved."

Gloria Steinem said, "We can tell our values by looking at our checkbook stubs." I'd like to add one to hers. You can learn a lot about a person's values by reading the bumper sticker on their car.

Character-building is a life-long process. It began in childhood when our parents and teachers taught us values--or didn't teach them to us. John Milton once said, "The childhood shows the man, as morning shows the day." True, who we are today did have its roots in childhood, but as adults, we have the option of continuing on in, or rejecting those qualities we learned.

Character is built as we reject the negative input in our lives and push on toward positive qualities and habits. Some come naturally to us. Perhaps, for you, it's being *friendly* or *honest* or *kind.* If so, all you need do is keep those virtues polished. Others qualities, though, don't come so naturally to us. In fact, it may be a down-right chore to even allow them in. Becoming aware of our lack of certain virtues, and desiring to have them, is the first step toward making them a regular part of our lives.

So what are some of these qualities about which we are speaking? You know them well: loyalty, courage, compassion, friendship, hard work, self-discipline, patience, perseverance and faithfulness. And then there's thoughtfulness, kindness, humility, honor, honesty, forgiveness, chastity, faith, hope, accountability and punctuality. And how about integrity, responsibility, tolerance, sensitivity, understanding, submission, neatness, creativity, humor, and a hundred more? Let's center in a little more closely on just a few of them.

Integrity. How do we develop this virtue? First, we set honorable and ethical standards and carefully live up to them.

We don't compromise our values. For instance, if profanity is offensive to us, we don't have to remain in the break room while someone is swearing like a drunken sailor. Without making a scene, we can simply excuse ourselves and leave.

Sometimes character commands that we stand alone when the crowd is going in another direction. We gain respect and help establish our integrity when we make our word our bond. If we promise to do something, we do it--even if it costs us something. It's so easy to make excuses: "I just didn't get to it." or "I forgot." or "I didn't know you still wanted me to do it."

Charles Givens in his superb book *SuperSelf* speaks about *faithfulness*. He says, "Your ability and willingness to keep your agreements is a direct measure of the level of control you have over your life." He adds, "Promise only what you can deliver and deliver what you promise." Givens tells that his life changed when he made a decision to keep all his agreements, and says ours will too.

He says, "Keeping your agreements builds trust and confidence in yourself and from others. When you keep your agreements, people know they can depend on you to do whatever you have said you will do. As a result," he continues, "your career moves faster, your business becomes more successful and your personal life is under your control. Your confidence increases as you discover that you can eliminate the obstacle, rather than break your commitment." He contends that "keeping your agreements is one of the most powerful *SuperSelf* tools you can apply in your quest to doubling your personal effectiveness."

One way we can let our integrity shine is by lifting others up with us. Maybe you've hosted a great community outreach, or you've produced an outstanding newsletter that has the community's admiration. Sure, you may have done most of the work yourself, but character in you recognizes all the little things others have contributed to the successful outcome. It makes them look good, and you are respected because you have not grabbed all the credit for yourself.

Honesty, too, plays a part in integrity. As a storekeeper, Abraham Lincoln once overcharged a lady a small amount. Realizing his mistake, he closed the store and took off on a two or three mile trek to return the small sum. My Dad was a man like that.

In 1962, when I got married, he and Mom bought fancy little aprons for the girls who would serve the cake. When we got home there were four of the dollar aprons in the package rather than the three he meant to purchase. Dad would not rest until the fourth one was paid for. It was a small thing, but it made an impression on my life and probably the store clerk's as well. Today I realize my father was a man of character, with the virtues of honesty and integrity shining brightly--even long after his death.

Let's look at **obedience** and **submission.** William Bennett in his terrific *Book of Virtues for Young People* tells that George Washington's mother was once asked how she raised such a fine son. Mrs. Washington was quick to reply, "I taught him obedience." For many of us, obedience, or submission, does not come easily. Yet we are under the authority of our employers and others. Being willing to submit to their wishes, when we'd rather do it our own way, is a mark of character. There may be times, though, when character prevents us from complying with their demands--like if we are asked to do something that is obviously wrong.

"Responsibility," says Bennett, "is the ability to accept the consequence of our actions and performance."

Accountability, like *responsibility,* is furthered when we quickly admit our mistakes, when we take full responsibility for our blunders. "I blew it. I should have been more sensitive to your feelings. Please forgive me. Let me treat you to breakfast tomorrow."

Henry Rogers in *Rogers Rules For Success* says, "If you look around, the person who assumes the blame is the most liked, the most respected, and the most admired. No one punishes him or humiliates him. He is trusted because he has the self-confidence and self-assurance to say, 'It's my fault.'"

Charity is an old-fashioned word. Webster defines it as, "love for one's fellow man," "leniency in judging others," and "generosity toward the needy." Charity (or love) may be one of those seemingly natural gifts that we don't even have to work at. But let me ask you again, "Are you as kind to yourself as you are to others?" We often forget that "charity begins at home."

Sir Thomas Browne in 1642 wrote these wise words: "But how shall we expect charity toward others when we are uncharitable to ourselves? 'Charity begins at home', is the voice of the world; yet is every man his greatest enemy and, as it were, his own executioner."

None of us enjoys *self-discipline* but it, probably as much any other virtue, will help us become the person we want to be. Charles Givens in *SuperSelf* writes, "Discipline is something you do, not something you have. You have the freedom to choose to act with discipline and decisiveness. To become what others refer to as a disciplined person requires only that you "do discipline" over and over as a conscious act until repetition makes discipline a subconscious habit. Doing discipline means that you choose not to allow fatigue or interruption to become an excuse for inaction or a change of plan."

Socrates once said, "Let him that would move the world, first move himself." It would be nice to have all the things we want NOW, to say the things we feel, to eat the foods we desire. But if we don't master our desires, they will master us.

William Bennett writes that self-discipline involves controlling the temper, the tongue, the appetite, and our wishes. (Whoops! I just ran upstairs for some frozen yogurt---but I'm working on it!) "It's recognizing your limits," he says, "not wanting things too soon. It's saying yes to the right things and no to the wrong things. It is taking charge of yourself."

We have numerous opportunities to develop the virtue of *patience*. You may have stolen a little time to tackle that stack of overdue charts or reports. But people keep coming into your office wanting to chat. Or, after a super busy day you are finally finished and heading for the door. A coworker comes up to you and wants a favor. It can be a real test of patience. I think you get the picture.

It's up to us to choose if we'll let character grow within us. We said earlier that character is who you are in the dark. For me, personally, success is wrapped up in being true to myself, in holding true to the Judeo-Christian values I hold dear, in striving to make that person I am in the dark, one with the person I show to the world. As we bring these two natures within us into one, we find a new freedom. We no longer have to be different things to different people. We gain a healthy new self-acceptance. And when we master ourselves, we are more in control of our lives.

Henry Rogers says, "Ability will get you to the top, but character will keep you there."

Ann Landers says, "Keep in mind that the true meaning of an individual is how he treats a person who can do him absolutely no good." And we often have opportunity to meet such people.

So why not welcome those sometimes trying situations as opportunities to grow in our various character qualities? And when you do, you won't be able to hide it--the character that's already in you will shine out even brighter for all the world to see.

CHAPTER 3

Recognizing and Developing Your Unique Gifts

Have you ever noticed how some things come easily for you while others are a downright struggle? Do you ever find your self-esteem plummeting because you can't sing like Mary, or do needlepoint like Pat, or speak in public like Gene? Do you ever feel that you may have been absent when gifts were being passed out? If so, you can take heart; you are not alone.

Ruth Van Reken in her article, "If you think You're Nothing Special, Think Again" featured in *Today's Christian Woman* (1) says, "Lots of people never do anything because they can't figure out how to do everything." And isn't that just like us? We assume we must be able to do everything and do it well. Consequently, we become frustrated when we fall short in some area.

Even the most self-confident of us probably, on occasion, feel ungifted. On a personal level, I absolutely love to put words together. I rejoice over a neatly-turned phrase, and I get enthused over a clever advertising campaign. But give me a set of numbers or a mathematical problem, and it's a real frustration. Oh, I'm as good as the next guy at math, but I find little enjoyment in it. I hate problem-solving but, thank goodness, my husband thrives on it. In fact, he makes his living at it. I am at ease speaking before hundreds of people, (the number one fear of most people, even over death) but when it comes to clapping my hands to music, I really struggle. Without a natural sense of rhythm, I have to watch someone else just to keep time. So what!

I've learned that one secret to excellence is in recognizing our strong points and functioning in those areas. Also, in allowing others who are gifted in our weak areas to pick up the slack and to shine in their areas of expertise. When we try to function outside our gifted area, we have minimum effectiveness and quickly become weary. It's like trying to fit a square peg into a round hole. When we operate within our accomplished scope, we feel challenged and refreshed and are highly productive.

Sometimes we overlook our gifts because they come so naturally to us. On the other hand, we may perceive gifts as those things that require struggling to achieve. But that's not the way it works.

You may be in a meeting where tension is running high. Your natural wit picks up a bit of humor in the situation. Without a second thought you crack a joke. Everyone laughs and the tension is broken. You think it's nothing, but look again.

Why didn't others use this wonderful tool of humor in just the way you did? Wasn't it because they lacked your gift? It comes so naturally to you. Because you enjoy finding the funny side of things and making people laugh, you may have overlooked your gift--a great sense of humor.

Give anyone a sheet of paper and ask them to list their short comings. Without hesitation, the page is quickly filled. Then ask them to list what they like about themselves and their particular gifts. They remain thoughtful and are reluctant to write. Many times we are the last to recognize our gifts.

My husband and I used to teach a *Married for Life* seminar in our home. Doing the homework one week, I was challenged to write down what I loved about Rick. I listed such things as his sense of humor, his humility, his gentleness, his telling me often that he loves me, his hugs, his encouragement, his humble attempts at being romantic. In less than an hour I had filled twelve pages with short phrases of things I loved about him. Yet when challenged to write a list of positive things about myself, I felt limited. But Rick found it easy to list my good qualities. If you are having trouble locating *your* gifts, ask someone who really cares to jot down some things they love about you. Then review their words and try again to make your own list of gifts. This is not a time for modesty. Be honest and your natural gifts will begin to surface.

Let's explore some foundational or motivational gifts. They have been written about by many experts [2][3][4][5]. These are inborn endowments that inspire, stimulate, incite, propel, and arouse us. Some of these gifts include *leadership, adminis-*

tration, organization, serving, exhortation, teaching, creativity, compassion, hospitality and *giving.* It's important to note that gifts also have a negative side. By becoming familiar with these natural gifts and their down side, we can better understand our coworkers, some who may occasionally prove to be "thorns in our flesh". As we learn about these gifts in operation, we may see that our areas of disagreement with others may simply be the negative side of their gifts at work. Let's take a more in-depth look at some specific gifts.

One with the gift of leadership sets goals and inspires others to voluntarily help him accomplish them. Taking charge and assuming responsibility comes natural to him. He sees the overall picture but often overlooks details.

The down side of this gift is that leaders can dominate a group and exercise control.

The gift of administration is the ability to clearly comprehend necessary goals and to formulate and carry out plans to reach those goals. Administrators (we're not referring here to facility administrators) are good at overseeing duties, delegating work, meeting deadlines, and are conscientious about details.

The down side is that administrators can come across as slave-drivers rather than facilitators.

Those with the gift of organization can visualize the "big" picture, and then define long-term goals. Organizers don't like to follow a predecessor's method; they must set their own goals and carry them out. They must organize that which they control. They like things efficient, systematic, and neat. They appear inexhaustible, enjoy meeting new people, and are good communicators. Since it is difficult for them to verbalize love or appreciation, they show it in their actions. Projects, to them, are like puzzles; they must find where each piece fits. It thrills them to have others enjoy their accomplishments.

The down side is that organizers may see people as resources, and projects may appear to be more important than people. Others can feel pressured by their drive to see things accomplished.

Characteristics of the gift of serving is the ability to quickly recognize unmet needs, and to remember particular likes and dislikes of others. They forget themselves and their weariness while meeting others' needs. They find it hard to refuse any request. They work in the present, wanting action *now*, not some long-term thought-out plan for the future.

The down side is that servers may feel unappreciated. They give so much, and it hurts when others don't recognize their effort. Since they respond so quickly in a situation, they may lack prudence in giving directions. They may also appear pushy and cause others to think they are trying to advance themselves.

Those with the gift of exhortation have a logical, organized mind with the ability to visualize. They like to see practical steps of action taken in a situation. Putting great emphasis on verbal communication, they exhort others. They can get up and speak easily and can remember conversations in great detail. Exhorters are people-pleasers and are sensitive to the reactions of others.

The down side of this gift is that exhorters may stretch the truth, and that they are quick to offer advice. Because of their organized nature which formulates step-by-step methods of procedure, they may seem to over-simplify problems. They may also stir others to action for personal gain.

Those having the gift of teaching (not necessarily teachers) put great importance on accuracy. They question their "teachers" in life, whoever they may be. To them, truth is authenticated through research which they love. They like that truth presented in a organized manner.

A negative aspect of the gift of teaching is missing the big picture while concentrating on details. Teachers may take pride in their knowledge and even boast of it. Because of the teacher's need to get at the truth, others may feel as if *their* ideas are being questioned.

Those with the gift of creativity have clever ideas and creative solutions to problems. Requiring freedom to work in their own manner, they quickly become frustrated with uncompromising thinkers. They are often misunderstood.

Because they don't fit into a strict mold, they may feel estranged in groups and may be reluctant to take an active part in group activity.

One with the gift of compassion feels deeply when others hurt, be it physical, mental, or emotional pain. They grieve when unkind words are spoken to anyone. They want to remove those hurts.

This gift has a definite down side. Since they are so sensitive to other's feelings, and because they quickly detect insincere motives, they may appear hard to get to know. In decision-making, they may appear "wishy-washy", and they may find it difficult to be firm when necessary.

Some people love to give. This may be the gift of giving in action. Givers are sensitive to needs that others may overlook. They give quietly and joyfully without being pressured. They want their gift to be of high quality. They are elated when their gift meets a particular need.

Some negative aspects can be pride in giving and an attempt to influence with their giving.

The gift of hospitality is a special ability to make others feel welcome. It offers food, shelter, and a warm inviting atmosphere to those in need.

One down side of this gift is that they may be taken advantage of, and then feel unappreciated.

There are so many wonderful gifts. As most people quickly comprehend, professional people are often uniquely gifted people. And you are no exception. Still, you may not feel that way because there are so many areas where you fall short.

Begin to search out your inborn, natural gifts. You may see yourself in one or more of the motivational gifts. You may recognize a natural talent for being organized, for decorating, singing, encouraging others, problem-solving, listening, friendliness, humor, appreciation, thoughtfulness, or numerous others. These are not small things. Sure, we all want to continue to stretch ourselves and learn new things, but by knowing what our gifts are *not,* we have a healthy new freedom to guiltlessly say "no" when demands outside our scope of expertise are placed upon us.

So forget about competing with those who excel in gifts that are not yours. It's no contest! Develop *your* gifts and let your unique personality and talents shine forth in your own areas. In other words, bloom where you are planted.

References:
(1) *Today's Christian Woman,* January/February 1996
(2) *Motivational Gifts,* Marilyn Hickey Ministries
(3) *Your Spiritual Gifts Can Help Your Church Grow* by C. Peter Wagnerin
(4) Bill Gothard advanced seminar materials
(5) Others

CHAPTER 4

Leadership Struggles: Leadership Solutions

You are a leader. Oh maybe you don't feel like a leader, but no matter how you slice it, you are constantly being thrust into leadership positions. But are you comfortable there? Is it an area in which you feel under-qualified? Or, on the other hand, do you possess *natural* leadership abilities? If so, would you like to sharpen those inherent skills even more? And if not, would you like to *have* those leadership abilities operating more freely in your daily life?

Well, rest assured, it can happen. Too often we erroneously label ourselves either "leader" or "follower" and leave no room in between for a modifier. Some say leaders are born, not made. We all, no doubt, know someone who appears to be a natural-born leader--someone we admire, respect, maybe even emulate, someone who has a way with people. When he (or she) leads, they willingly and happily follow. He is strong, likable, decisive, and caring.

What makes one a leader, anyway? Is a leader only the top person of an organization, business or team? Or are there levels of leadership? What are the qualities of a successful leader? Can one who is not a "born" leader become an "effective" leader? Let's explore that issue a bit and see how it applies to our professions.

True, some people are blessed with an innate leadership ability. Yet each of you have qualities and responsibilities that set you apart as a leader. Just look about you. Perhaps you lead a department. Maybe you lead certain daily activities. You may lead a paid or volunteer staff. You lead fellow workers to participate in some of your programs. And you may lead fund-raising campaigns.

In addition to all that, you may have special leadership gifts. You may be able to see the big picture while others are hung up on details. You may be gifted to keep meetings on track when a discussion wanders away from the point of the meeting. You may have a knack for peacemaking. You may have communication skills that allow you to represent your facility as a spokesperson. You may be adept at motivating people, including coworkers. You may be able to see the humor in, and get people laughing at unpleasant company happenings.

And once you leave your job for the day, no doubt you have a home and family to lead. Perhaps you are a leader in your church, your child's school, in sports, or in some club or organization. It may not be as the president, but perhaps as chairman of the refreshment committee for a PTA party, or as base umpire for your child's softball team. Since you are regularly looked to for leadership (whether you like it or not), why not brush up on some of those needed skills.

What does it mean to be a leader? Being a leader, to me, first consists of knowing yourself and being willing to let others know the "real" you. It involves recognizing your unique giftings, developing them, and sharing them. It means listening to and learning from personal criticism. It means being willing to shoulder the blame even when you may not be personally responsible. It involves being bold enough to stand up for, and stand alone if necessary, to support the values you hold dear.

My husband, Rick, a "born" leader, was quick to define a leader as "one who compels followship, one who foresees the near future happenings and formulates a plan to deal with them; one who inspires others to catch the vision and run with him." He went on to say, "Teddy Roosevelt would lay buried on San Juan Hill had he not inspired the Rough Riders to follow him up the hill and to fight with him." That's the way we define leadership and being true to oneself. Let's look at what some well-known leaders have to say on the subject.

* Dale Carnegie, Mr Leadership himself, told the story of two great composers, *Berlin* and *Gershwin*. (1) When they first met, Berlin was already famous but Gershwin was still a struggling composer earning just $35 a week. Berlin was impressed with Gershwin's talent so he offered Gershwin a job as his musical secretary for $100 a week. (A real temptation, no doubt.) But he then surprised Gershwin recommending he

not accept the generous offer. He cautioned Gershwin that if he took it he might become a second-rate Berlin. Berlin's advice to Gershwin was to keep on being himself so that someday he might become a first-rate Gershwin. Gershwin took the elder's advice and went on to great success with Broadway musicals. One of his best known works was his 1935 hit, *Porgy and Bess.*

* Steve Forbes, the multi-millionaire who ran for President in 1996, also advises us to step out of a shadow and be ourselves. He says, "Imitation leads to an early grave because it's not you. When my father died, people said, 'How can you fill his shoes?' My response: 'He was like a great athlete. You retire his number, retire his shoes, and build your own shoes.'"

* General Eisenhower once demonstrated the art of leadership in this way. He put a piece of string on the table and said to the men around him: "Pull it and it will follow you anywhere; push it and it will go nowhere. It's the same with people."

* General Patton said, "Never tell people how to do things. Tell them what to do and they will surprise you with their ingenuity."

* President Harry Truman, in his natural down-home manner, had this to say: "A leader is a man who has the ability to get other people to do what they don't want to do, and like it!"

A leader *leads*. Not only does he (or she) lead, he makes leaders out of his followers. He does this by investing in his people, by treating them with respect, by helping them see how their jobs relate to the organization as a whole. Lao-Tzu described a leader this way: "A leader is best when people barely know he exists. When his work is done, his aim fulfilled, they will say: 'We did it ourselves.'"

Successful leaders provide a vision. When they are enthused, their vision can be "caught" by those who work with them. Then they allow their subordinates some freedom in deciding how to carry out that vision. After giving them general guidelines, the leader backs off and lets the workers find the most creative way to achieve the desired outcome. This requires trust on the part of the leader.

You may be responsible for a big party coming up and know just what you want to do. A trusted volunteer suggests that she can handle most of it for you. You are so weighted down with other responsibilities, and you are truly grateful. But you are apprehensive, too. *Can she do it as well as you?* After some consideration, you give her the go-ahead. You tell her your plans and what you hope to accomplish, then you pull back and let her take over. Of course you are always available for consultation--if requested.

The party may not be done exactly the way you would have done it, but it did come off. And by letting go of the total responsibility, you have accomplished three things: You've bought yourself extra time since much work was lifted from your shoulders; you've sharpened your leadership skills by delegating; and you are mentoring the volunteer to become a leader herself.

Still, letting go of the reigns requires trust on your part. Remember micro-managing is not giving others the opportunity to develop. You hold them down by constantly making all the little decisions.

Ralph Waldo Emerson said, "Trust men, and they will be true to you; treat them greatly, and they will show themselves great."

In a survey of 15,000 people, as published in *Credibility: How Leaders Gain and Lose it, Why People Demand It* written by James Kouzes and Barry Posner, the most important trait to effective leadership was "honesty" receiving 87% of the vote. And it was followed by other vital traits: being forward looking (having a vision)--71%; being inspirational--68%; and being competent--58%. The authors go on to say that "honest people have credibility, and that's what gives leaders the trust and confidence of their people."

Without trust subordinates will not follow you. *Communications Briefings* in their July 1996 issue say, "Don't expect people to follow you only because your title says they should. To enjoy real authority you have to earn your followers trust and respect. To do so be honest, share information openly, and be as quick to deliver the good news as you are the bad. Also, be willing to admit why you are wrong, and never break a promise." By trusting them, even if they make mistakes, and they will, you are building leadership into them. Leaders free others to be who they really are. They encourage subordinates to grow and to think for themselves.

James Stockdale once said, "Strange as it sounds, great leaders gain authority by giving it away."

As I suggested earlier in my perception of leadership, leaders generally have a strong sense of values. Some qualities found in successful leaders are trust and honesty, persistence, fairness, decisiveness and a positive attitude. They are also good listeners, good communicators, and goal-setters. They believe in the inherent self-worth of others. They let their subordinates know exactly what is expected of them. They are visible and approachable. Of course not all leaders can have all these qualities, so the next best thing is for them to associate with peers who have the qualities they lack. Let's look a little more closely at those and other winning qualities.

A discipline for organizing their time and their priorities is usually found in the successful leader. Their goal-centeredness allows them to tackle important matters first and, if time permits, deal with less important matters. Persistence inspires the leader not to give up easily when frustrating obstacles arise. A sense of humor helps, too. Communication abilities are apparent in confident speaking, and the ability to always look on the positive side of things; also in seeing a situation through the other person's eyes. Leaders generally listen 70% of the time and speak 30%. And when they do speak, though they frequently have good vocabularies, they use short, clear sentences. No matter how busy they are, they always make time to communicate with their people.

Decisiveness, with the ability to take some risks, is another vital quality of leaders. As professionals, we certainly need to be decisive. Many situations require a quick response. Quick, not rash, decision-making reduces unnecessary stress. The author of *Executive Excellence,* recommends that we set tight deadlines and push for quicker decisions from our subordinates. He says, "Let them know you will tolerate honest mistakes but not inaction and inertia." Leaders hold themselves accountable by carefully examining themselves each day and the decisions they have made. If they've made a wrong decision, they either live with it and learn from it, or they do what's necessary to correct it. Either way they've been decisive and have not let themselves hang in the balance of indecision.

Have you ever noticed in a conversation that the person asking questions is generally the one in control? People tend to respond when questions are asked. Good leaders use this tactic, too. They direct the conversation with questions: "In what way?" "What do you expect will be the result?" "Can you tell me...?" "How much do you anticipate it would cost?" Rick regularly uses this technique. People love it because they see he is interested in their opinions and ideas. By asking questions, he not only helps them feel worthwhile, but he assists them in sorting out their own thoughts, whether their plan or idea is feasible or not. And when they come to the conclusion themselves, the vision becomes more defined and their enthusiasm rises; or they see for themselves it's not a workable plan at all.

As leaders, we can become role models to our volunteers, our staff, and those about us. We can challenge *them* to become leaders themselves by using the question method. Charles Manz and Henry Sims in their book *Super Leadership*(2) show how to direct by asking questions:

To further self-observation the authors recommend asking such questions as: "Do you know how well you are doing?" "How about keeping a record of how many times that happens?"

To facilitate self-set goals, they ask: "How many will you shoot for?" "When do you want to have it finished?" or "What will your target be?"

To promote self-evaluation leading to self-reinforcement, they suggest asking: "How do you think you did?" "Are you pleased with the way it went?" "Why don't you try it out?" and "Let's practice that."

To further cognitive-focused self-leadership, Manz and Sims suggest you ask: "How do you like your job?" "Have you thought about trying different work methods that you might enjoy more?" "What opportunities do you see in the current problem you face?"

I'm sure you can see how leadership skills apply to you in your profession. Think again of the many areas which you direct. You are not called a professional director without good reason. A director is a leader, no matter how large or small their scope of leadership. You may have a staff of 100 or 12, or just two volunteers, or none at all. You may still have a department to lead, and you need to constantly sharpen your leadership skills.

Lee Iacocca offers a word of advice: "Never rest on your oars as a boss. If you do, the whole company (or department) starts sinking."

We can hone those skills by observing executives and other leaders in action. *What positive qualities do they possess?* You can practice delegating. You can actively work at molding those under you into leaders. You can practice your listening skills. You can read good books on leadership. You can step out of any over-cautious zone and take more risks. You can be the best leader possible in whatever area of leadership you are relegated. And when those particular skills become visible, those about you will, no doubt, determine that you indeed are a "born" leader.

References
1) *The Leader in You, How to Win Friends and Influence People and Succeed in a Changing World*, by Dale Carnegie & Associates, Stuart Levine and Michael Crom.
2) *Super-Leadership*, Charles Manz and Henry Sims

Other Sources
* *SuperSelf*, by Charles Givens
* *Overcoming Indecision*, by Theodore Rubin
* *Leadership*, William Safire, Leonard Safir
* *Taking Charge*, by Perry Smith

CHAPTER 5

The Benefit of Failure

Have you ever felt like a failure? Maybe at the moment, no. Things are going great--at your company, in your profession, in your personal life. But if we are really honest, most of us would have to admit that at some point in our lives we have felt like a failure. Maybe you didn't get a coveted job. Maybe you flunked a college course. Maybe you blew your exercise program. Maybe your recent state survey was a disaster. But is that all bad? Surprisingly NO! Someone once said, "Success is failure turned inside out."

Dr. Alan Goldberg appropriately said, "Failure, rejection, and mistakes are the perfect stepping stones to success." Everyone one we know as successful was once a failure. Let's look at some of them.

This man wasn't rich, in fact he was down-right poor. He had little education but a lot of perseverance. As he grew up, he held many common-laborer-type jobs: farmhand, deckhand, store clerk, mailman. After getting fired from one job, he decided to go into business for himself. But he failed at that, too, because he liked to tell stories better than working. His lack of success, though, didn't bother him; he was in love--and happy beyond belief. Then disaster struck. His beloved fiance died, and he was broken. Friends feared he might commit suicide. He suffered bouts of depression throughout his life.

Gradually this man pulled himself back up. He met and married another woman. Perhaps the relationship lacked the intensity of his first love, but it was acceptable. Being a poor man, their first home was above a tavern. Before long they began a family, but tragically, three of their children died during their childhood. Not succeeding at much in his life, the man decided to try politics. His resume may have looked like this:

> He failed in business in '31.
> Defeated for the Legislature in '32.
> Failed again in business in '32.
> Ran for Speaker in '38. Lost.
> Ran for Elector in '40. Lost
> Ran for Congress in '43. Defeated.
> Ran for Senate in '55. Defeated.
> Ran for Vice Presidency in '58. Lost.

Would you consider this man a failure? It seems everything that he tried failed. If any man ever felt like a failure, he must have. Well before you answer, let me tell you, as Paul Harvey says, "the rest of the story." I told you his first home was above a tavern. Well, his last home was the White house. In 1860 he ran for President of the United States and won. His name was Abraham Lincoln.

Joan Crawford, at one time, was considered by the theaters owners of America, a failure. Louis B. Mayer, of MGM Studios, fired her after many years of working for him. Knowing she had once been a sensation, she refused to quit. She convinced Warner Brothers that she was right for the lead role in *Mildred Pierce*. *And she* won an Academy Award for it! Sometime later, Crawford returned to MGM and was a real asset to the studio.

Likewise, Clark Gable once insisted on the role of an Irish statesman in the move *Parnell*. The movie was a disaster. Gable didn't give up. He landed the role of Rhett Butler in Gone *with the Wind* which thrust him into perpetual movie fame. He loved acting. Lewis Lawes said, "Never give a man up until he has failed at something he likes."

Lee Iacocca was fired by Henry Ford as president of Ford Motor Company. Iacocca refused to think of himself as a failure. He took his lemons and "made lemonade," so to speak. Before long, he took over the leadership of Chrysler and brought the nearly bankrupt company into prosperity.

Michael Jordan must have been devastated when he was cut from his high school basketball team. But he would not accept that. His name is now a household word. Whately said, "He only is exempt from failures who makes no efforts."

Walter Cronkite applied for a job as a radio announcer but was told he'd never make it as an announcer. He didn't accept that as failure. How many years did we watch him as anchorman on the nightly news? Someone once said, "There is no failure except in no longer trying." We have many opportunities to experience failure. But do we give up? Of course not. We are professionals and we are not quitters. We take the negatives and turn them into positives.

Bill Cosby said, "I don't know the key to success, but the key to failure is trying to please everybody."

Richard Nixon said in 1971, "I think perhaps as I look back at those who shaped my own life--and there are a great deal of similarities between the game of football and the game of politics--that I learned a great deal from a football coach who not only taught his players how to win but also taught them that when you lose you don't quit, that when you lose, you fight the harder the next time."

"When a setback hits us personally, our first impulse is to become so emotionally upset that we fail to learn the lesson," says David Schwartz in *Thinking Big*. He says, "Don't run away from mistakes, seek out faults and try to correct them." When we have a failure we should ask ourselves two questions:

1) What is the worst thing that could happen in this situation?
2) What can I learn from this?

When a bad situation is thrust upon us and we ask what is the worst thing that could happen (I might lose my job in the down-sizing), a certain release comes. "Okay," we say, "I was looking for a job when I got this one. I can do it again." Then determine, on paper, what you can learn from the situation. Thus, we can take a negative happening and learn from it. We can turn it over and over in our minds to see what lesson is hidden in the situation.

Keats said, "Failure is, in a sense, the highway to success, in as much as every discovery of what is false leads us to seek earnestly after what is true, and every fresh experience points out some form or error which we shall afterward carefully avoid.

"Striking out means you are in there swinging," says Henry Rogers in *Rogers Rules for Success.* Babe Ruth struck out 1330 times but he hit 714 home runs. In the major leagues, when players come up to bat, 40% of the time they make it only to first base. We must expect some failure on our way to success.

Bovee said, "A failure establishes only this, that our determination to succeed was not strong enough."

I love this failure story. Dr. Norman Vincent Peale, while in his 50's, became totally frustrated while attempting to get a book manuscript published. Publisher after publisher rejected it. Finally, feeling like a failure, he threw it in the trash. His wife Ruth believed strongly in him and started to dig it out. He forbade her to take it out of the wastebasket. The next day Ruth went to still another publisher with a strangely-shaped brown paper-wrapped package in her hand. Placing it on his desk, the publisher opened the package, surprised to find a wastebasket filled with a manuscript. She would not disobey her husband who had forbid her to take it out of the trash, but knowing he had something worthwhile there, she acted without his knowledge.

That manuscript became the book, *The Power of Positive Thinking*, which has sold millions of copies and has encouraged untold people worldwide.

Dowden said, "Sometimes a noble failure serves the world as faithfully as a distinguished success." Let's look at a few others the world might have temporarily labeled "failures:"

* Thomas S. Monaghan, the founder of Domino's Pizza had his share of failure. Buying a pizza parlor while still in college, he soon added a second one. Financial problems quickly mounted. A bad partnership dragged it down in 1965. In 1968, a severe fire for which insurance covered only 10%, pulled the company further down. A creditor, the bank, took over the management of the chain in 1970. But Monaghan refused to concede failure. He resumed control 10 months later facing over $1.5 million in debt and a hundred law suits against him. He focused on his simple mission statement: to deliver a quality pizza, hot, within 30 minutes, at a fair price. In 1990, Domino's sales were near $2 billion. (1)

* R.C. Macy failed seven times before his store in New York became successful.

* English novelist John Creasey got 752 rejection slips before he published 564 books.

* Andrew Carnegie, attended school only four years. A poor Scottish lad, he began his working career for just two cents an hour. He eventually gave away $365 million.

* Louisa May Alcott, author of Little Women was counseled by her family to become a seamstress or a domestic.

* Henry Ford frustrated his dad by showing no interest in farming. He just wanted to "fix things" in the tool shed.

* Vince Lombardi the famous football coach had an expert say of him, "He possesses minimal football knowledge. Lacks motivation."

* When Thomas Edison had tried 1000 times to make the incandescent light bulb he was encouraged to quit. Refusing, he said, "Now we know 1000 things that don't work."

"I never did anything worth doing by accident," said Edison, "nor did any of my inventions come by accident; they came by work."

Dr. David Schwartz, in his splendid book *Thinking Big* gives these five guideposts to help you turn defeat into victory.

1) Study setbacks to pave your way to success. When you lose, learn, and then go on to win next time.

2) **Have the courage to be your own constructive critic.** Seek out your faults and weaknesses and then correct them. This makes you a professional.

3) **Stop blaming luck.** Research each setback. Find out what went wrong. Remember, blaming luck never got anyone where he wanted to go.

4) **Blend persistence with experimentation.** Stay with your goal but don't beat your head against a stone wall. Try new approaches. Experiment.

5) **Remember, there is a good side in every situation.** Find it. See the good side and whip discouragement.

You can indeed take heart hearing about these successes of others. Sure, there may be times when you feel like a failure, but look at all negative circumstances as stepping stones on the road to success.

Farar said, "There is only one real failure in life that is possible, and that is, not to be true to the best one knows."

And A.B. Alcott said, "We mount to heaven mostly on the ruins of our cherished schemes, finding our failures were successes.

1) Recorded in *Timing is Everything* by Denis Waitley

CHAPTER 6

Attitude Begins With You

Life is a choice. We can be happy, or we can be sad. We can complain, or we can approve. We can stand still, or we can act. We can choose to be a victim, or we can become an overcomer. We can opt to keep a bad habit, or we can lay it down. We can be stressed out, or we can take one day at a time. We can react, or we can respond. The choices we make, day in and day out, all add up and create our attitude--our attitude toward those in our care, toward coworkers, toward family and friends, and toward life in general.

Charles Swindoll is quoted by Zig Ziglar in *Over the Top* as saying: "The longer I live, the more I realize the impact of attitude on life. Attitude, to me, is more important than facts. It is more important than the past, than education, than money, than circumstances, than failures, than success, than what other people think or say or do. It is more important than appearance, gifted ability, or skill. It will make or break a company, a church, a home. The remarkable thing is we have a choice every day regarding the attitude we will embrace from that day," he continues. "We cannot change our past, we cannot change the fact that people will act in a certain way. We cannot change the inevitable. The only thing that we can do is play on the one string that we have, and this string is, attitude. I am convinced that life is ten percent what happens to me, and 90 percent how I react to it. And so it is with you...WE ARE IN CHARGE OF OUR ATTITUDES."

When I was visiting a church in Florida a couple years ago, I heard a really neat story about attitudes in the preacher's sermon. He said he found it on the internet. I have not been able to locate the author to properly credit him or her for it. So with my compliments to the author, here it is:

Jerry was the kind of guy you love to hate. He was always in a good mood and had something positive to say. When someone would ask him how he was doing, he would reply, "If I were any better, I would be twins." He was a unique manager because he had several waiters who had followed him around from restaurant to restaurant. The reason the 20 waiters followed Jerry was because of his attitude. He was a natural motivator. If an employee was having a bad day, Jerry was there telling him how to look on the positive side of the situation. Seeing his style really made me curious, so one day I went up to Jerry and I asked him, 'You can't be a positive person all of the time; how do you do it?'

Jerry replied, "Each morning I wake up and say to myself: "Jerry, you have two choices today. You can choose to be in a good mood, or you can choose to be in a bad mood. I choose to be in a good mood. Each time something bad happens, I can choose to be a victim, or I can choose to learn from it. I choose to learn from it. Every time someone comes to me complaining, I can choose to accept their complaining, or I can point out the positive side of life. I choose the positive side of life."

"Yeah, really? It's not that easy," I protested.

"Yes it is," Jerry said. "Life is all about choices. When you cut away all the junk, every situation is a choice. You choose how to react to situations. You choose how people will affect your mood. You choose to be in a good mood or a bad mood. The bottom line is: It's your choice how you live life."

I reflected on what Jerry said. Soon, thereafter, I left the restaurant establishment to start my own business. I lost touch with Jerry, but I often thought about him when I made a choice about life instead of reacting to it.

Several years later, I heard that Jerry did something you are never supposed to do in the restaurant business. He left the back door open early one morning and was held up at gun point by three armed robbers. While trying to open the safe, his hand, shaking from nervousness, slipped off the combination, and the robbers panicked and shot him. Luckily, Jerry was found fairly quickly and rushed to the local trauma center. After 18 hours of surgery and weeks and weeks of intensive care, Jerry was released from the hospital with fragments of bullets still in his body. I saw Jerry about six months after the accident. When I asked him how he was, he said, "Any better and I'd be twins. Want to see my scars?" I declined to see his wounds, but I did ask him what had gone through his mind when the robbery took place. "The first thing that went through my mind was that I should have locked the back door," Jerry replied. Then, as I lay on the floor, I remembered I had two choices. I could choose to live or I could choose to die. I chose to live."

"Weren't you scared? Did you lose consciousness?" I asked.

"The paramedics were great. They kept telling me I was going to be fine. But when they wheeled me into the emergency room and I saw the expressions on the doctors' and nurses' faces, I read, 'He's a dead man.' I knew I needed to take action."

"What did you do?" I asked.

"Well, there was a big burley nurse shouting questions at me," said Jerry. She asked me if I was allergic to anything. 'Yes!' I replied. The doctors and nurses stopped working as they waited for my reply. I took a deep breath and yelled 'NEGATIVITY!' I'm choosing to live. Operate on me as if I am alive, not dead."

Jerry lived, thanks to the skill of the doctors but also because of his amazing attitude. I learned that every day we have a choice to live fully. Attitude, after all, is everything.

It would be wonderful if all our coworkers were like Jerry. Life would be so much easier. Unfortunately, it doesn't work that way. Too many people struggle with attitude problems. We can't change anyone else's attitudes, but we can work on our own. We can decide to "respond" to situations rather than "react" to them. Even if we don't feel the way we would like to feel, we can change our actions, and then our feelings will follow those actions. Zig Ziglar in the above-mentioned book shares this story that proves the point:

Two women worked together and absolutely detested their jobs. Without other job prospects in sight, they both decided to quit without notice on Friday of the next week. With that decided, they talked and laughed and joked with each other about what they were about to do. On the day they were to leave, they went in an hour early, made coffee, and tidied up the place. When the first coworker arrived, they graciously served her coffee and treated her like royalty. They did the same for each of the following coworkers. Everyone wondered what was going on.

The culprits just laughed between themselves and said that since everyone had been so nice to them, they were going to turn the tables. When the customers began arriving, the two schemers greeted each customer warmly, cheerfully, and enthusiastically. They were there to serve, and did it graciously. The rest of the employees watched in shock at the change in the two who had so hated their jobs just the day before. At 4:30 one asked the other if they were going to walk out and not say anything, or if they were going to make a grand exit and tell coworkers that they'd never see them again.

"What are you talking about?" said her partner in crime.

"Well, you know we are quitting today," reminded the other.

Her partner said, "Quitting! Are you kidding--quitting the best job where I have had the most fun I've ever had in my life? No way!"

Zig points out that the circumstances of the job had not changed. Only their attitudes. Their attitudes changed because their actions changed. He says, "When you don't really want to, or feel like doing what needs to be done--do it, and then you will feel like doing it."

Someone said, "Attitude is a starting place. Attitude is our inner disposition toward God and toward others, even toward ourselves. Our attitude determines what we will do with what God has given us."

Norman Vincent Peale in *The Power of Positive Thinking* encourages us to "take a piece of paper and make a list, not of all the factors that are *against* you, but of those that are *for* you. If you or I or anybody think constantly of the forces that seem to be against us, we will build them up into a power far beyond that which is justified. They will assume a formidable strength which they do not actually possess. But if, on the contrary, you mentally visualize and affirm and reaffirm your assets and keep your thoughts on them emphasizing them to the fullest extent, you will rise out of any difficulty regardless of what it may be. Your inner powers will reassert themselves, and with the help of God, lift you from defeat to victory."

I'm sure you all remember the classic fable about the sun and wind arguing who could make the man down below take off his coat. The wind boasted he had the power to do it so he went first. He blew hard, and the man buttoned his coat. He blew harder and harder. The man drew his coat even closer around him. Finally, he blew with all his might, and the man would not remove his coat. It was the sun's turn. He gently peeked through the clouds. The man unbuttoned his coat. He shined a little brighter and without any encouragement, the man removed his coat and threw it on his shoulder. And so it is with our attitudes. We can growl and throw our authority around, but as most professional people know, a kind word works so much better and faster.

Stephen Arterburn in *Winning at Work Without Losing at Love* says the "The only thing winners are up against is their own attitude." He says, "What you think you are up against is not what you are up against." How often do we look at our circumstances and think they justify our mood? We're sick, we're broke, our kids are in trouble, the list goes on and on.

Atterburn makes his point by sharing the story of Joni Eareckson Tada who as a teenager dove into a pool and became paralyzed from the neck down. She felt sure her dreams of being a writer and illustrator were gone forever.

Though she could have focused on all her adversity, she changed her attitude realizing some people were better off than she, and some were worse off. She even married after her accident. Joni, through her strong faith in God, learned how to paint by holding a brush between her teeth. She has written and illustrated books, painted greeting cards, spoken to thousands of people, and written and recorded songs. Through her radio program, she works to collect wheelchairs for disabled people in poor countries. Her program is one of my favorites because she is such an encourager. Though Joni could have despaired and found herself in a nursing home or mental institution, she directed her attitude toward her abilities not what she had lost.

In *Succeed and Grow Rich Through Persuasion,* Napoleon Hill and E. Harold Kewon write, "Every adversity carries within it the seed of an equivalent or greater benefit. If we can capture this truth and can accept the fact that this universe is governed by immutable laws which are part of a creative force, no matter how difficult it may be to see the reason--then we can ride out any storm which besets our lives. Your attitude in a time of adversity determines much of its eternal effects on your life--for good or ill."

So how does all this apply to you? Well, first off, attitudes are highly contagious. If someone comes to work cranky, soon other staff members, and eventually those under your care pick up the grumpy attitude. But you can break that cycle. Good attitudes are contagious, too. They are caught, not taught. Let's look at some ways to keep our attitudes positive.

1) **Determine you will be the sunshine in your company,** not the storm.

2) **Look for the good in others.** You may have to look deeply, but somewhere in that complaining person, you will find a good feature to build on and to encourage him or her about.

3) **Look for something good in every negative situation.** Ask, "What can I learn from this? How can I use it to become a better, stronger person?"

4) **Make a list of all the things you like about your job,** your boss, your company, your coworkers, your community, your mate, your family, your church, and your friends. Read it over regularly, and when unpleasant situations arise, focus on those positive things.

5) **Before you speak, stop and think if anyone will be hurt** by your words.

6) **Again, *respond* rather than *react*.** Listen carefully to the whole story before you answer. Then speak softly, slowly, and thoughtfully.

7) **Listen to yourself,** even if it means carrying a tiny tape recorder around with you for a week. Eliminate the negative talk from your vocabulary.

8) **Feed yourself positive self-talk.** "Well, it looks like another tough situation has arisen. But I am strong and I

have a good sense of humor. I know I can handle it in a way in which no one will be hurt. I am good at this sort of thing."

9) Be enthusiastic about whatever you do. Feelings follow actions.

10) Deal gently with others' faults.

11) Remember, in every situation, you have a choice to make. Why not choose the positive one?

As Ziglar says, "A positive attitude starts with you. Once you develop, maintain and apply that attitude, life's inconsistencies won't have the power to disrupt your positive outlook."

It's not easy to keep your chin up, to keep smiling when things go wrong, to answer in a positive manner, but *you* can do it because you are a professional!

CHAPTER 7

Polishing Your People-Pleasing Power

Would you like to spread sunshine wherever your go? No doubt you already do bring brightness into many lives. Rather than the negative stressful situations, we are going to now look at the positive side. We're going to discuss the many things that we can do to bring out the best in others and, subsequently, to spread good will within our company, our home, and our community.

You are each unique individuals. God doesn't make junk. Sure you've all had negative things happen in your lives, and they may have caused you to feel badly about yourselves or to be more aware of certain weaknesses: you're too indecisive, too slow, too quick to speak, too cautious. You're impatient, you're pushy, you're unorganized. So what! No one's perfect.

Concentrate on the qualities you *do* have. Refuse to verbally or even mentally put yourself down. Don't ever say, "I'm so clumsy." "I'm forgetful." or "I'm too fat." Your subconscious believes as fact what you tell it, and you will begin to act upon the message you speak. Try writing yourself positive reinforcement notes, in the first-person, that state what you *want* to be. Read them several times a day:

* I am a very graceful person and I always walk with poise.
* I am a loving and understanding person, and
* I can get along with anyone.
* I weigh 125 pounds (or whatever weight you choose to be), and I look and feel great.
* I am superb at my job, and I am liked by all those with whom I work.

As we said before, be your own best friend. There's always someone to put you down so don't join the band wagon. When negative thoughts cross your mind, replace them with your positive confessions like those above. It takes 21 days to form a habit. If you keep this up, soon you'll find yourself with a new, positive way of thinking.

Next, take stalk of your strong points: a ready smile, an encouraging attitude, a generous nature--or being a peacemaker, an organizer, an earnest listener, a good speaker, whatever. As we discussed in chapter three, if you haven't already, why not take a moment now and make a list, without modesty, of every positive quality you possess. When your list is complete, choose two each week, and work on developing those gifts even more. Once you are aware of your own distinctiveness, you can begin to share that sunshine with others. So how do you start?

First, regard the other person as more important than yourself. Discuss subjects that interest him. When President Theodore Roosevelt was going to meet with a man, he would stay up late the night before and read up on subjects which were of interest to his visitor. No matter what their position in life, ask other's advice.

Socrates once said, "One thing I know, and that is that I know nothing."

We can learn something from anyone. I once had an 87-year-old friend, Otto. He showed up at my door years ago when my children were small and endeared himself to us all. Otto had a scant third grade school education, yet he taught me valuable things that I would not have known otherwise: a colt's legs at birth are almost as long as they'll ever be; and a tree grows from the top, the lower branches will always remain the same distance from the ground as when planted; and that my carefully-selected strawberry plants were really wild ones that would barely produce. Otto was a simple man, but he had wisdom to share.

Everyone needs to feel important, maybe not for importance sake alone, but simply to know they are accepted and loved. There are many ways we can encourage others to feel good about themselves. One is to pay sincere compliments. You've heard "flattery will get you everywhere." No! I'm not advocating cheap flattery, but rather sincere compliments that will help the other person see his own value.

Once I was in a bank having a car loan processed. I was seated across the desk from a lady who was busy writing. Suddenly she looked up and commented, "You know, you are a neat lady!" Startled, I replied something like, "I beg your pardon." She continued, "Ever so often someone comes across my path who impresses me. And I tell them so." Then she went back to her writing. "Thanks!" was all I could mutter. But you know, that lady taught me a lesson in spreading sunshine. I have followed her lead. When someone impresses me, I take the time to tell them, "You know, you are really a neat lady (or gentleman)." I don't know how freely the banker uses it, but to me, this is not a casual compliment; I save it for rare and special people. And I hope those people pass the process on to someone else who can pass it on to yet another someone. People need to be appreciated.

When our children were at home, I delighted in occasionally surprising one or another of them or my hubby with a "because I love you gift." It was never much--something I picked up on sale, a freebie, something given to me, or something I found at a garage sale. And they loved it!

A gift when there's no real occasion is more treasured. We often think of giving to those we love. Try giving to someone who's "a thorn in your flesh." Take a cold soft drink or a donated flower in a small vase to a coworker who is not a fan of yours. If she asks why you're giving it to her say, "Just because you're a nice person." Maybe no one ever said that to her. Rent a movie your child's been wanting to see and pick up some microwave popcorn. Curl up on the couch and watch it with him. Place some flavored tea bags in a mug and visit an elderly neighbor. Share a cup of tea together.

If you're passing a greeting card counter and see one that reminds you of someone, buy it and surprise them. A brief phone call to a co-worker who's home sick says, "I care about you." Take a cup of coffee to an overworked staff member who's too busy for a break. Drop a love note in your sweetie's lunch bag, briefcase, or pants pocket. If your child arrives home before you, tape a note to the refrigerator, "Jimmy, look in the cookie jar." In it, place a reassuring note of love and his favorite cookies. You'll indeed be spreading sunshine.

Take breaks. No, of course you don't have the time, but studies show that workers who do are more productive. But the reason I recommend breaks is not necessarily to be more productive, but to get to know the staff better and for them to get to know you. Unfortunately, people who don't take breaks are sometimes perceived as stand-offish when that is the furthest thing from their mind. They are just too busy to stop. But co-workers who *do* take breaks may not see it that way. Schedule your time, some days, to spend a few minutes in the break room chatting with, but even more, listening to co-workers chat. Refuse, though, to take part in company gossip. Successful people can't afford that luxury. Let them know you up close, not just as a professional, but as one who's approachable and who is interested in them.

Rejoice with those who rejoice and weep with those who weep. Acknowledge other's successes. Extend your hand, smile, and sincerely rejoice with a coworker who has received a promotion, or who has just announced her engagement, or whose child has just won a softball tourney. Clip newspaper articles of other's successes, and send them to the recipient with a little note of praise. If their child is sick, they are being laid off, or they've been reprimanded by their boss, empathize with their feelings and offer a kind word, a note, or a simple gift.

One of the best ways to win friends and spread sunshine is by listening. Listen actively and encourage others to talk about themselves. Look the speaker in the eye. Ask questions if needed to clarify what he says. Don't feel you have to have input in every conversation. Think before you speak. At meetings talk less and listen more. Look behind the words being spoken to the intent of the speaker. What exactly is he trying to communicate? By listening actively, you are being observed as a good conversationalist.

In conversations, put other people at ease. To learn how, watch people you admire who make you feel that way. Notice their manner. Do they ask questions, smile, look you directly in the eye, speak softly, talk little? Learn from successful conversationalists. Even if they personally hold a different stance on an issue, they try to see your side. Also, good communication is often furthered by copying the other person's body language. If they lean back in a chair, fold their arms in front of them, open their arms, smile, frown, or whatever, inconspicuously mimic their gesture. Salesmen are well aware of this useful tool.

Make notes about happenings in the lives of coworkers and others to which you may wish to respond. You might even create a "Because I Care" notebook to record this information. Under their names, add spouse's name, children's names and ages, birthdays, favorite color, hobbies, good things happening in their lives, or any particular burdens they are carrying. Jot down facts as you learn them. Imagine how surprised Mary in housekeeping will be when her daughter receives a card from you for her Confirmation. People want to be remembered.

Put to memory the names of the staff and other people you meet. Dale Carnegie in his wonderful book, *How To Win Friends and Influence People* wrote about a beloved salesman and politician, Jim Farley. Farley asked Carnegie what he thought was the reason for his (Farley's) success. Carnegie said, "I hear you can call ten-thousand people by their first names." Jim said, "No. You are wrong. I call fifty-thousand people by their first names." In conversations, Carnegie would inconspicuously find out the speaker's birthday and say it over and over until he could slip away and write it down. Then he'd send them cards on their special day.

In disagreements, likable people hear both sides and don't take a position. They focus on the problem, not the person. They don't try to win an argument. Carnegie says, "You can't win an argument. You can't because if you lose it, you lose it. If you win it, you lose it because you hurt another person's pride."

Be willing to volunteer if you possibly can. "Sure I'll bring cookies to the staff meeting." or "Yes, I'll be glad to take notes." People notice and admire those who are quick to respond when a need is mentioned. Be trustworthy. If you say you'll do something, be faithful. A department head that I worked with always wrote little notes if she promised to do or bring anything, and stuck them in her pocket. "I'll bring you that article out of the paper tomorrow." And she would do it. She was trustworthy.

There are so many more ways to earnestly please people and spread sunshine. Be faithful to your word, keep your promises. Give credit where credit is due. Don't hog the praise, pass it around. Answer calls and respond to needs quickly. Involve staff in your activities. Admit when you don't know the answer, but promise to find it and get back to them. Then do it. Refuse to take up an offense against someone. Never hold grudges. If you do a newsletter, feature one staff member each month. Be a coach and encourage others to be all they can be.

Not everyone can handle the above assignment--to forget themselves and please others--because they may be too much into themselves. But you can because you are a professional, and professionals have broad shoulders. They are givers and they love people. They like to please and to spread sunshine wherever they go. Sunshine brings light and warmth and comfort. And you are indeed that sunshine to your company.

CHAPTER 8

Patiently Prevailing Over Procrastination

You're tired. It's been a tough day at your company and you want to go home. How nice it will feel, you fantasize, to sit down in your easy chair, and for five or ten minutes, prop your feet up. Then when that magical moment arrives, rest doesn't come. You notice a stack of unanswered mail on the table demanding attention, and bills that need to be paid. You close your eyes to ignore them, but your mind will not relax. You think about all the things at work you've been putting off: making fund-raising phone calls, improving the volunteer program, having a heart-to-heart with your assistant who has not been measuring up. Then your mate arrives home: "Honey have you sent for that free information on vacation spots yet?" he (or she) asks. You haven't.

Then Junior approaches, "Mom, when are you going to make my chocolate chip cookies? You promised you would soon," "he whines, "but soon never comes!" or "Dad, you promised you'd play catch with me. Come on!"

It can be frustrating to say the least. You have so many things to be done, and so little time. You just want to forget it all. It's so easy to understand how one can slip into the role of a procrastinator.

First, lets look at what procrastination is, and is not. Procrastination means "to put off until later; to delay doing something that you know deep down you really should do." There are a zillion reasons for procrastinating: You may be afraid to tackle the job; it may seem too big to handle. You may be waiting for someone else to take it off your hands. You may hope it will just go away. You may find the task too boring or too unpleasant. Maybe it requires skills or tools you do not have available.

Experts say one of the main reasons people procrastinate is fear--fear of failure, fear of the unknown, fear of exposing themselves, fear of pain, fear of change, and even more, fear of success. It's easier not to perform some tasks, they think, than face up to the fear.

But is it always procrastination when you don't get to something that needs doing? Absolutely not. There's a difference between procrastination and prioritization. Let me give you an example:

I'm an avid garage saler. That's what I do for fun, and for a break from the lonely life of a writer. I like antiques. Some time ago, I found an old-time oak washstand--you know, the kind with a drawer, and towel rack on the back. It was in bad condition, but I like the challenge of restoring the old to "good-as-new." So I stole a little time from my overcrowded schedule and went to work stripping the finish. I detest leaving any project half-done. But--I was in the final stages of my book, *Activities Encyclopedia*. To meet the deadline, I had to concentrate all my energy on it. Never the less, I brought the unfinished washstand into my living room, put a doily on it, and set some small antiques on it. Every time I walked by, I was reminded of that unfinished task. And I was bothered by it. I couldn't wait to get back to it. But the book had to be finished first. That was not procrastination. That was prioritization. For me, getting that washstand sanded and varnished was a reward for finishing the book (and I eventually did!). Do you see what I mean?

You've all heard the saying, "Never put off until tomorrow what you can do today." The chronic procrastinator's motto might be "Never do today what you can put off until tomorrow." I've jokingly used it myself. Most of us procrastinate at some time or another.

When I am researching something I'm going to write, I usually also pick my husband's brain. This time I pumped, "Honey, do you think you are a procrastinator? And, if so, how do you procrastinate?" He thought long and hard. Finally, he said in his own unique humorous way, "I procrastinate getting out of bed in the morning!"

For some of us, though, procrastination is not an occasional happening but has become a way of life, a bad habit. We put off making that necessary phone call, shopping for needed supplies, balancing the checkbook, making a doctor's appointment, or making a decision. We delay getting the oil changed in the car, cleaning out the gutters, cleaning the bathroom, starting an exercise program, or improving our spiritual life. We even make excuses for ourselves: "Oh, that's just my nature. My mom was a procrastinator."

Sometimes we put things off until something else happens: "I'll do it when my assistant shapes up." or "When the kids leave home, I'll wallpaper." or "When the new year comes, I'll start my diet."

How do we procrastinate? The ways are endless. For me, it's running upstairs from my basement office to get a cup of tea or an unneeded snack, or perhaps to throw a load of clothes in the dryer when I'm supposed to be writing. For you, it may thumbing through a new supply catalog, calling a friend, running errands, or chatting too long with an interesting client.

How often do we, instead of tackling a chore, convince ourselves that we really do need to kick back and relax? Other times we put off getting started until there's no longer time to accomplish the task.

For instance: Maybe we're going to paint the living room. We hunt for the lost paint brush. Then we have to find where hubby (or wife) left the drop cloth. We get the paint open and realize the roller is worn out. We run to the store for a new one. We meet a friend there and decide to have a cup of coffee together. When we get home we realize we need to make a phone call. By that time we look at the clock and decide there's no use starting now. It will have to wait until another day.

So what can we do if we find ourselves procrastinating? First, we need to ask ourselves why we are procrastinating. Is it fear? Is the job too big? Do I feel inadequate to handle it? Is the job distasteful? Am I afraid of failing at it? or succeeding at it? Edwin Bliss in his book, *Doing It Now* says, "If you can pin down the cause of your procrastination, you will have taken a big step toward overcoming it and replacing it with the habit of prompt action."

Procrastination wastes energy, energy that could better be applied to a needed task. When we procrastinate, we fail to live up to our potential. Cervantes once said, "By the streets of by and by we arrive at the house of never."

Successful people seldom procrastinate. They are movers. They get things done, personally or by delegating--even those unpleasant chores they may dread to do.

Overcoming procrastination involves self-discipline. Self-discipline is the ability to delay gratification. Ray Kroc, the man who lifted the *McDonald's* hamburger to its fame, says "The longer I live the more importance I attach to a man's ability to manage and discipline himself. The man with the capacity for self-discipline can tell himself to do the truly important thing first. Therefore, if there is not enough time to go around and something must be neglected, it will be the least essential task." (1)

Dr. Joyce Brothers in her book, *Positive Plus, The Practical Plan For Liking Yourself Better*, encourages making a "procrastination list." On it list everything you put off and never seem to get around to--answering a letter, sewing on a button, asking your boss for a raise. Brother's says when your list is complete, prioritize the jobs according to importance. To determine importance ask yourself, for each item on the list, "What is the worst thing that would happen if I didn't balance my check book? clean the refrigerator? return that phone call?" Dr. Brothers recommends each day doing three things on your procrastination list. Then enjoy crossing them off. She says to start off with a job you don't like to do. When that is completed, allow yourself to do the easiest job on your list next.

In her own life, to avoid procrastination, Brothers says she keeps three baskets, the first for urgent matters: make plane reservations, give a lecture, finalize a T.V. appearance. Her second basket is for important, but not quite so urgent items-- pay bills, make appointments, get hair done. Her third basket is large like a bushel basket. In it goes everything else. She goes through it when time permits and again at the end of the year when she discards much of it. She recommends the procrastination list be kept for at least eight weeks or until the habit of procrastination has been broken.

Patricia H. Sprinkle, author of *Women Who Do Too Much:* "Stress and the Myth of the Superwoman," advises this tactic to get a tough job done. Ask, "Is it unpleasant?" "What unpleasantness will it entail?" "How bad will it be?" Then she says to walk through the entire unpleasantness in your mind. Ask, "How long will the unpleasantness last?" She recommends when you start the task that you check the clock and promise yourself, "By such and such a time, it will all be over." She also says you can set a timer and try to complete it in that length of time. In addition, she advises saying to yourself, "I will work 30 minutes on this task today, and then I may quit." All that is well and good, you might say, but is there anything else we can do to overcome the habit of procrastination? There certainly is.

1) First, make a decision. I will not procrastinate without first examining why I am doing it. Don't focus on procrastination itself, but on the task at hand. Determine if you can delegate the unwanted task. Perhaps you can pay someone else to do it while you spend your time more productively.

2) Carry a small notebook on your person at all times. Write down things you promise to do, or things you need to do, rather than trying to remember, but then forgetting. Remember, "The smallest pencil is better than the longest memory."

3) Promise yourself a reward. "When I finish this job, I can rent a movie and relax for a couple of hours." Remind yourself frequently of the reward that awaits you on completion of the task.

4) Realize that not all jobs have to be done perfectly. That saying, "Whatever is worth doing is worth doing well" goes only so far. Some things are just not that important.

5) Decide in advance how long each task on your list will take. You'll probably have some 10-minute jobs, 20-minute jobs, 3-hour jobs, maybe even some 3-day jobs. Allow enough time for the job or situation you need to attend to. Often we speculate that we can do a job in less time than it really takes. There may not be time to tackle something big today, but you may be able to complete a 10-minute job while you're waiting for your next activity to begin.

6) Break a big job down into manageable segments. Perhaps you've gotten behind on your documentation. Decide that today you will do one-fourth of those overdue charts. "By the mile it's a trial, but inch by inch it's a cinch."

7) Make starting easy. The night before, psych yourself up to do the hardest task the next day. Think it through and decide what you'll need to accomplish it. Gather those items and/or the needed information. Choose a time when you are fresh and unpressured to do the chore.

8) Be prepared. Put in your car those things that need to be returned or dropped off somewhere, so when you're in the area you can do it. Keep reading material in your car, too.

Carry an emergency box in your vehicle filled with anything you might need from a postage stamp to an earring back to a screw driver. When you find yourself caught by a train or having to wait till the kids get out of school, you're prepared. You can use the time to make a list of items to pick up at the hardware or grocery store, work on memorizing something, or jot off a note to Aunt Martha. Even while waiting at traffic lights, I read little bits and pieces of articles.

9) Use your calendar to write reminder notes of jobs you've been putting off: *Get help lined up for the picnic.* Write notes to yourself and put them where you'll see them often. Ed Bliss (2) suggests using a tape recorder and giving yourself a pep talk. Then play your message back to yourself when you need to hear it.

10) Set deadlines for yourself and for others if their procrastinating is reflecting on your performance. For instance, if your boss has been putting off looking over your newsletter before he gives the okay to print it, you might say (in an nice way, of course), "This is already past the printer's deadline, so if I haven't heard from you by Friday, I'll assume it's acceptable as is." As the old saying goes, "Nothing improves procrastination like deadlines."

11) Tell friends you are trying to overcome your habit of procrastination. Ask them to hold you accountable.

12) **Find a role model,** someone who accomplishes much and seems to have their life in order. Ask questions and learn from them.

13) **If nothing else works, perhaps the job is not worth doing** or is something you shouldn't do. Ask what would happen if you didn't do it. Paul and Sarah Edwards in *Working From Home* write, "Sometimes procrastination is a warning signal, a way to tell yourself 'this is not the right thing to do' or that it is a waste of time and doesn't need doing."

The Edwards' tell the story of a potter who kept putting off delivering a sold pot. "She wanted to take a picture of it first," she said. Finally, the potter came to the realization that the reason she wasn't delivering the pot was because she really wanted to keep it. So she called the buyer and worked out an alternate plan. Another tip the Edwards' give is, "When, for whatever reason, you find that you continue to avoid tasks, identify what you're doing instead, and cut off the escape routes."

When it comes right down to it, for most everyone, there's always more to do than there are hours in the day. As I've gotten older, I realize even more that I have to say "no" to the *good* things so I can say "yes" to the *best* things. In other words, I have to decide carefully what really needs to be done, and what I really want to accomplish. And I have to say no to many things I would choose to do if time permitted.

You may have heard the quote, "You can't go on repeating the same things and expect a different result." And that's the way it is with procrastination. But the good news is, "We don't have to remain procrastinators." We can rise above that inauspicious habit, and when we do, our self-esteem will rise right along with us. Because once we have overcome procrastination, we are well on the road to success.

(1) Quoted in *Doing it Now* by Edwin Bliss
(2) *Doing It Now*
(3) Other publications

CHAPTER 9

The Power of the Spoken Word

Perhaps you remember that little childhood chant: "Sticks and stones can break my bones but words can never hurt me." Unless one has a constitution made of steel, though, it seems to be an untrue statement. Words have power. They can hurt and heal, accuse and acquit, build up and tear down, cause sadness, and bring joy. There are words of deceit and words of truth, words of blessing and words of cursing, words of rebuke and words of encouragement, words of complacency and words of restlessness.

Words take so many forms. There are words of bondage and words of freedom, words of fear and words of security, words of cowardice and words of bravery. There are also words of regret and words of satisfaction, words of warmth and words of coldness, words of love and words of hate, words of life and words of death.

Nathan Hale spoke a word of honor when he said, "I regret that I have but one life to lose for my country."

John F. Kennedy spoke a word of challenge when he said, "Ask not what your country can do for you, but what you can do for your country."

Douglas MacArthur, during the World War II, when he was recalled and had to leave his troops behind in the Phillipines, spoke to his men a word of promise: "I shall return!"

When a policeman says "Stop!" we know it is a word of authority backed up by the uniform he wears. Doctors pronounce words of life and words of death: "You'll live to be 100." or "You have six months to live." And how often do we pronounce words of sickness upon ourselves? "I think I'm getting a cold." or "I feel like my back is going out." or "With all the pressure, I'll probably end up with a migraine." We claim diseases, "*My* asthma is acting up." or "*My* arthritis is bad." I once read a book entitled, *What You Say Is What You Get.* And I find that it is so true. Once I verbalize a potential illness, I seem much more likely to get it than if I speak a word of health: "I'm as healthy as a horse. Most bugs just pass me by."

There are words that make us feel dirty (such as a pervert might say), and words that make us feel clean (like an old hymn sung at church). There are words that bring confusion and words that bring clarity. Have you ever stopped to ask for directions and come away more confused than you were before? And then the next person you asked made those directions perfectly clear?

There are truthful words and lying words. There are sincere compliments and insincere words meant only to flatter. Oprah Winfrey did a TV show recently on lying. It was amazing how many people felt that it is okay to lie--if it makes other people feel good. They would say things like, "Your hair looks great." when they really hated it, or "That's a neat dress." when they were thinking how unattractive it was.

There are mature words flowing from a rich word-stock, and baby words coming from extremely limited vocabularies. When my grandson, Collin, was just 20-month old, he wanted so badly to communicate. And he found a way to do it with just 80 or so words. I often sent him packages via UPS. Whenever he saw a UPS truck, he pointed to it and said "Mam-maw!" or "Thanks Mam-maw." I used to joke, that sometimes I've carried a few extra pounds, but I've never been described as a UPS truck. But until he had developed a rich and full vocabulary, that was okay with me.

In our professions we have no choice. We must use words constantly. But what an opportunity! We, with our words, can create, command, energize, encourage, and challenge everyone with whom we come in contact. We can help them learn, grow, and feel good about themselves. Words are potent and can be so marvelous.

Anna Hempstead Branch said, "God wove a web of loveliness, of clouds and stars and birds, but made not anything at all so beautiful as words."

Tyron Edwards understands the power of the spoken word: "Words are both better and worse than thoughts; they express them, add to them; they give them power for good or evil; they start them on an endless flight; for instruction and comfort and blessing, or for injury and sorrow and ruin."

Frederika Bremer spoke about the sorrow part. "There are words that sever more than sharp swords; there are words the point of which sting the heart through the course of a whole life." We've probably all, through the careless use of words, been hurt badly by someone. But just as words split relationships apart, they can also be used to heal them. Our words tell so much about us. Jesus Christ, the greatest teacher who ever lived, declared "...the mouth speaks what the heart is full of."

Emerson put it this way: "A man cannot speak but he judges and reveals himself. With his will or against his will, he draws his portrait to the eye of others by every word. Every opinion reacts on him who utters it."

Much of how we respond to situations has to do with our upbringing. When I was rearing my children, I found this little poem published in Abbey Press. Now my daughter, who's raising a young family, keeps it handy.

> If a child lives with criticism, he learns to condemn.
> If a child lives with hostility, he learns to fight.
> If a child lives with ridicule, he learns to be shy.
> If a child lives with shame, he learns to feel guilty.
> If a child lives with tolerance, he learns to be patient.

If a child lives with encouragement, he learns confidence.
If a child lives with praise, he learns to appreciate.
If a child lives with fairness, he learns justice.
If a child lives with security, he learns to have faith.
If a child lives with approval, he learns to like himself.
If a child lives with acceptance and friendship, he learns to find love in the world.

It would be a wonderful world, indeed, if we had all grown up with encouragement, praise, fairness, security, approval, acceptance, and friendship. Then perhaps we would all know how to speak words which edify rather than tear down. But, unfortunately, many of us were raised with criticism, hostility, ridicule and shame. And those words and attitudes, learned so many moons ago, still have a way of slipping out of our mouths, much to our dislike. And, even if we grew up in a home where we received positive feedback, we may still sometimes say hurtful things.

Gary Smalley, author, speaker, and marriage counselor, says that men speak about 10,000 words a day while women speak 25,000. We women frequently use ten words to say what a man will say in one. That's good! Our speech may be more colorful, more explanatory. But, the more we speak, the greater chance we have of slipping up with our words, of saying something we wish we hadn't.

Roscommon said, "What you keep by you, you may change and mend; but words, once spoken, can never be recalled."

Gossip is like that. I once heard gossip described as a feather pillow that is taken to the top of a high hill on a windy day.

There it is split open and dumped out. The feathers blow everywhere. No matter how hard one might try, they could never determine where those feathers might land. And if the person changed his or her mind after the they had spilled them, they also could never, ever recover every feather.

It's been said that God gave us two ears and one mouth so we could listen twice as much as we speak. Shakespeare said, "When words are scarce, they are seldom spent in vain." And wise Solomon said, "Seest thou a man that is hasty in his words? There is more hope of a fool than of him."

Still, I don't know about you, but I love to talk. In fact, I get paid to talk. I have a favorite saying: "How do I know what I think until I hear what I have to say?"

My husband, Rick, who is slow to speak, assembles his thoughts together in his head before speaking them out. He's valued by others and listened to because when he does speak he has something worthwhile to say. Still, Rick feels he misses many opportunities, because of his delayed, thoughtful response, to say the things he would really like to communicate. He feels that for some people of few words, like himself (many times these are men), it can be sort of a curse to have to communicate verbally. It's not that these folks don't have a great vocabulary--they may well--but they have difficulty expressing themselves quickly and being able to make their point before someone else jumps in and starts talking.

In 1924, Benjamin Cardozo wrote, "The search is for the just word, the happy phrase, that will give expression to the thought, but somehow the thought itself is transfigured by the phrase when found."

When we can't find the words to adequately express our feelings, body language can help. A hug, a touch of the hand, or a warm smile can speak volumes (see chapter 10).

Unlike Rick's method, I like to get my thoughts out and organized on paper, or speak about them to Rick or a trusted friend. Then I can better understand those thoughts and my true feelings about things. So I'm guilty of using many words.

How about you? As professionals it is difficult not to. So what can we do to protect ourselves from saying things we later wish we hadn't? Here are nine suggestions we may want to try.

1) Before we speak a single word, determine if anyone will be hurt by it. If so, refrain from using it, or rephrase it so as not to offend.

2) Next, think positively rather than negatively. We can look for something good in every situation we encounter, and in each person's remarks. We can ignore that pressing urge to respond unkindly even though we have been spoken to in a thoughtless way.

3) So what if we grew up with critical, ridiculing parents or parents who were loud, unfair, or who didn't offer the acceptance we desperately needed. That is all behind us now. As Rick says, "Just because we had an anchor placed on us doesn't mean we have to be dragged down by it. We can float it. We may not be able walk on water, but we can swim through life's problems rather than sink in them."

We don't have to allow that learned tendency to behave in a certain manner to continue in our lives. We can begin to confess things in the positive. "I believe I'm up to that challenge!" "I expect today will be a great day!" "I love rain; it makes things so green." "I know I can lose a pound this week." Work hard to put those negative confessions behind you. Remember, it takes 21 days to make a habit. Chart on the calendar today your decision to speak only positive words, and practice it earnestly for three weeks, or as long as is needed. No doubt, you'll soon notice real progress being made.

4) We can use kind words to offer others that acceptance, praise, fairness, security, and approval we received, or didn't receive, while growing up. Not only will we be raising the recipient's self-esteem, we will feel better about ourselves.

5) The book of Proverbs in the Bible, with many of the proverbs written by Solomon, is full of wisdom regarding the use of words.

6) Make friends with positive people. Attitudes are caught not taught.

7) Make an effort to smile more often. It's hard to speak negatively when you are smiling.

8) Be sincere in all your words, and in your compliments. Determine to tell the truth. It's better *not* to receive a compliment than to receive an insincere one. And there are always creative ways to comment without lying.

Recently a friend of mine changed a long-standing hairstyle. I really didn't like it much, but when I first saw it, I exclaimed in surprise, "Sally, you got your hair cut!" She, like most people, received it as a compliment. The fact that we notice can make someone's day. If someone wears an outfit you don't like, yet you feel a response is in order, you might say, "Susie, you look bright and cheerful today (if it is true).

9) Use the right words. Denis Cauvier in *How to Keep Your Staff Productive and Happy* says, "Remembering to use these six words--*clear, mean, honest, feel, direct,* and *want* -- can help you communicate better: Be *clear* by saying exactly what you *mean*. Be *honest* by saying what you *feel*. And be *direct* by saying what you *want*."

Words are indeed marvelous. I've heard Bible translators tell of going into tribal villages where there is no written language. They tell of the delight the natives feel when they see, for the first time, their own language written on paper. And there's so much joy and satisfaction when they can finally read those words. Our language is so full, so rich. We can communicate so many things with it. Pearl Bailey said, "You can taste a word."

Ralph Ellison said, "They [words] sing. They hurt. They teach. They sanctify. They were man's first immeasurable feat of magic. They liberated us from ignorance and our barbarous past."

For all of us, sincere words, when used properly, are like jewels. They are precious, colorful, and sparkling. They are beautiful to behold. And as they carefully flow from our mouths, they can be a priceless gift, a rich blessing to our staff, our volunteers, and those under our care. They can make the difference for someone, between a good day and a bad day. They can bring light and hope to a troubled heart. They can bring a smile to a sad face. They can bring poetry to a downhearted soul. And they can bring music to our own heart. Our voices and our language are indeed wonderful treasures. Let's use them to make life a little brighter for as many people as we can.

CHAPTER 10

The Gift of Listening

Want to *really* know what's happening in your company and in the lives of your coworkers? Want to know people on a deeper level? Want to be thought a good conversationalist? Want to have more friends? No doubt we all do. So what's the solution?

It can be summed up in a word: *Listen.* "Oh, come on now," you say. "It sounds so simple!" It does, but it's not. Listening does not come natural to most of us. Surprisingly, people in general, rate themselves as better listeners than they actually are. Oh, the intention of our hearts are good. We care about people and *want* to give them our undivided attention when they speak--but there are so many distractions. We've probably all met a few really good listeners, but for most of us, there's still room for improvement. Thank goodness, listening is a *learned* art.

Since 75% to 85% of our waking hours are spent communicating, and half of that time is spent listening, we have lots of opportunity to practice our hearing skills. Art

Linkletter, the famous TV interviewer, had a knack for pulling the most interesting words out of the mouths of children. He credits his unique interviewing ability to listening. He says, "Giving someone the compliment of your total attention enhances the quality of your personal relationship and can almost hypnotize the other person so that you can expect the best, most intimate answers, and the most interesting conversations that you've ever had in your life."

Listening is the ability to tune in to what another person is trying to communicate. It means shutting out, briefly, the numerous distractions about us and concentrating not only the words being spoken, but on the thoughts, the intent, and the feelings behind those words. True listening says, "I care. You are valuable. What you have to say is important to me."

Kevin Murphy in *Effective Listening* describes the craft in this way: "Listening is the accurate perception of what's being communicated. It is the art of separating fact from statement, innuendo, and accusation. It begins when one hears or observes what is being said, continues as one stores and correlates the information, then begins again with one's reactions. Listening is not the simple ability to decode information; it is a two-way exchange in which both parties involved are always being receptive to the thoughts, ideas, and emotions of the other."

As we said, listening doesn't come natural; it goes contrary to our human nature. We would rather express ourselves and our views than to hear another's thoughts and opinions. Learning good listening skills takes time. Maybe we can better understand positive listening by first exploring some negative habits that may have crept into our communication styles.

The estimated speed of thought moves four to five times faster than the speed of speech. Consequently, it is easy for our minds to wander or begin to think about a point on which we disagree. Also, there's a grand temptation to jump into the conversation prematurely without first letting the speaker have his say. Our unwelcome intrusion can sidetrack or even discourage him from making his point. When we talk, we don't listen, and when we don't listen, we're not learning or understanding what the speaker is trying to convey.

Eavesdrop on a few conversations. How often does one person try to outdo the other by telling a bigger or better story? Example:

First speaker: "I'm worn out. I've had so little sleep lately. My wife, Jenny, was just about recovered from a terrible bout with pneumonia when she fell and broke her leg. I've been carrying both our loads with the house, and the kids, and working to boot!

Second speaker intrusively jumps into the conversation: "Well, that's nothing! When my wife slipped on the ice last winter and was flat on her back for three months, three of our kids broke out with chicken pox--all at once! I had to take vacation just to take care of them all! I couldn't wait to get back to work. It about killed me!

The first speaker didn't want to be reminded that someone else had experienced worse problems; he wanted a little compassion and understanding.

Most of us hold at least some strong opinions on subjects close to our hearts. When someone shares an opposing view, we may feel compelled to jump in and "correct" his or her thinking. By doing this we let our prejudice stand in the way of hearing, and this prevents us from seeing the total picture. And, unfortunately, we can even make an enemy if we're not careful.

Another handicap to active listening is talking "at" people rather than "to" them. Suppose you work in a health care facility. Picture a resident interrupting while you are in the midst of a care-plan meeting, or while you are busy charting in your office.

"Minnie," you might say only half-looking up from your involvement, "I'm busy now. We'll take care of it later. Okay?" And though you are very busy, and though you spoke kindly, the resident might go away feeling she has been talked "at" but not really addressed. She may also feel rejected.

Many untrained listeners respond before they have all the facts. Successful individuals are often known to be givers. They are also fixers and quick responders. Subsequently, it's easy to find them "acting" without really "hearing."

Still another obstacle to listening is finishing sentences for the speaker. I, for one, am guilty of this. Before researching this chapter, I honestly thought that I was helping a person by providing a word when he would grope for the right one to express his thought. I thought I was showing him attention, compassion, and understanding. In reality, I learned this practice tends to frustrate the speaker and lessen his desire to communicate with us.

Sometimes we're too busy to listen, or we're just plain not interested in what the speaker has to say. Yet good manners prompts us to feign interest. Let's say you are frantically preparing for a company party. Guests will be arriving soon. Another good friend calls. It's a slow day for her, and she wants to pick your brain a bit. You care about her and don't want to cut her short, but you've so much to do. You only partially listen while you go on pulling needed items from the cupboard and directing staff and volunteers with hand gestures. It's an easy trap to fall into. Partial or false listeners are easy to spot. Oh, they may give the appearance of listening, but if they hear another more interesting conversation nearby, you'll notice them being distracted from your words.

Here's an example: You're at a party and a gentleman asks about your job. Loving it, you begin to share excitedly. Two men standing nearby are engrossed in a conversation about sports. You realize your listener isn't really tuned in to you anymore but is more interested in the sports conversation. He may even try to fool you that he is listening by throwing in an, "Is that so?" or "I see what you mean." or "Interesting." Kevin Murphy in *Effective Listening* says if you suspect someone is not really listening, respond to their "Interesting!" comment by saying, "Oh, do you find that interesting? What in particular about it interests you?" He says the false listener will know you are on to him and will begin to listen up.

So what specifically can we do to improve our listening skills? It doesn't take an expert to know that most people's favorite subject is themselves. To become a good listener, we must realize that people talk to fulfill a need. They may need to sort out their feelings. They may need to be listened to. They may need to be taken seriously. They may need help or advice. They may need to share some exciting news. They may need to find agreement for their opinion. They may need to present facts. They may need to get a laugh, which in turn builds their self-esteem. Whatever their need, just recognizing it hidden there behind their words will make active listening easier.

We need to catch ourselves in the act of poor listening. We might pretend we are a bystander and observe our conversational style. We need to quiz ourselves: *Are we really listening? Are we jumping into the conversation too soon? Are we finishing sentences for others? Do we only half-listen? Are we listening beyond the words to understand the content and to determine the speaker's need and his or her feelings? Are we getting all the facts before we speak?*

Try this exercise: Go away from several conversations and try to write down everything the speaker said. How much do you remember? The less you talk, the more you will hear.

Since nonverbals carry 55% of our message, we need to watch our actions. Perhaps we're not interested in a conversation so we let our eyes wander from the speaker. Or we look at our watch during the conversation conveying that we are too busy to listen. It's recommended that we look at our watch *before* the speaker starts. Tell her you are on a tight schedule now but really want to hear what she has to say. Decide on a time to meet. Make a note in her presence and keep the appointment.

Once we are aware of our weak areas, we can get serious about listening. We can count to ten and think before we speak. We can bite our tongue, if necessary, and ask ourselves if what we have to say is really important. If our mind drifts, ask the speaker to repeat what she said and then concentrate. Or summarize her words back to her, and then ask questions to better understand her message. By limiting our words and giving the speaker the gift of our full attention, we can render the emotional strokes she may be seeking.

People are drawn to individuals who are interested in what *they* have to say. Listeners are liked. By listening, we earn the right to be heard ourselves. And when we *do* speak, our words are given serious consideration.

True listening can open many doors. We'll see others opening up more to us. We'll see staff putting their trust in us. We'll better understand our employer's responsibilities. We'll see our meetings running smoother. We'll find ourselves more aware of what's really going on in the company, and hopefully we'll be more compassionate to the needs of those we work with. And, finally, we'll discover a new self-respect as we refrain from talking to let others have *their* say.

Carl Menniger once said: "Listening is a magnetic and strange thing, a creative force. The friends who listen to us are the ones we move toward, and we want to sit in their radius. When we are listened to, it creates in us, makes us unfold and expand."

And if we feel so good when we are listened to, why not share the gift with those about us? Let's give them the priceless gift of a sincere listening ear.

CHAPTER 11

Your Body Has a Language Of Its Own

If you were to go in to work one day, and at mid-morning for some reason you could no longer hear, what would you do? Would you panic that you could not communicate with co-workers? Tragic as that would be, you may find that *wordless* communication is not all that difficult.

We all speak two languages whether we are aware of it or not. There's our native language and a nonverbal language. We communicate with our words, sure, but also with our voice tone, voice inflections, eyes, face, smile, and body movement. My hubby, Rick, used to jokingly say, "Don't look at me in that tone of voice."

Without their uttering a word, we can determine whether a person is weak or authoritative, dependable or unreliable, trustworthy or suspicious, aggressive or passive, agreeable or unpleasant. Experts say that body language is more honest and more accurate than words. Psychologist Albert Mehrabian in his book *Silent Messages* says that our actions override our words. The messages we silently send out may contradict what we say. He says, "They are more potent than the words we speak. When our verbal messages are inconsistent with our body language, our credibility crumbles because most people will believe the nonverbal."

Even Shakespeare knew about body language. He wrote, "There's language in her eye, her cheek, her lip. Nay her foot speaks; her wanton spirits leak out at every joint and motive of her body."

The old colloquialism is indeed true: "Actions speak louder than words." Surprisingly, according to one study (1), only 7% of the message we send is transmitted with words (2). Fifty-five percent is sent visually--our gestures and our body language, and 38% is vocal, the way we say it. This involves the tone of our voice, the speed with which we speak, the inflections, the pauses, and the sighs.

To a successful person, understanding body language is vital. It can enhance our professionalism, improve our relationships with coworkers, and help us better understand people with whom we must deal.

Just last week my husband and I went to the nursing home to help with a weekly service our church holds there. One delightful and alert lady, Bertha, can say only one word. She responds to any question or comment with "Never. Never. Never. Never. Never." Bertha loves the service, but this time when I went looking for her, she had just been tucked in for the night. When I inquired about her attending the service, her reply was the same as always: "Never. Never. Never." But her body language screamed something else. Her eyes pleaded. "Get me up! Get me up!" Much to her delight, the kind nurses did just that. You may know or work with someone like Bertha who cannot communicate with words, so it's vital that you understand their non-verbal language.

Think of some of the common body language we use every day: the handshake, the nod, the pat, waving, shaking the head, smiling, crossing the legs, blowing a kiss, folding the arms across the chest. How about scratching the head, rubbing the neck, shrugging the shoulders, and shaking a fist? Then there's tapping the fingers on a table, twiddling the thumbs, steepling the fingers, and wrinkling the nose. There's sticking the chin out (or the tongue), cocking the head, puckering the lips, licking the lips, and biting the lips. And how about covering the mouth, crossing the fingers, crossing the legs, and looking at someone sideways? But what does it all mean?

Much body language is self-explanatory, but some is a little more obscure. We all know fingers are crossed for luck, and that we wave for greetings and for separations. We shake our head up and down for yes, and side to side for no. We recognize an outstretched chin as a sign of antagonism, pursed lips as disagreement, and a policeman's raised arm and open palm to mean "halt!"

Licking the lips indicates anxiousness, and biting the lip, self-criticism. Rubbing the palm is a sign of eagerness, anxiousness, or anticipation. Thumb-twiddling, finger-tapping, and tapping the foot implies a lack of attention, impatience, or aggravation. Touching one's face might indicate the person is thinking about what you have said. Clenched fists communicate "I'm afraid." Fidgeting, head propped up on the hand, or sighing can mean "I'm bored".

Crossing the legs and folding the arms across the chest is a protective gesture. It may say "Don't bother me." Or it could mean the person disagrees with you, is feeling defensive, or needs to be convinced. We scratch our head when we are trying to make a decision. We rub our neck or eyes and pull at our chin when we are undecided, unconcerned, distrustful, or feel we've lost control. We squint when we see something repugnant. We shrug our shoulders to say "I don't know." or "Who cares?"

When we look at someone sideways, we are saying we don't trust that person. When we tilt our head sideways, we may be listening intently or showing understanding or compassion. High-caste people tilt their heads back more than low-caste people. It may seem insulting. Remember the old saying, "to look down one's nose at someone?" Signs that could indicate "Get lost" or "I'm not interested" are: body odor, beards, mustaches, a hairdo that covers the face, gloomy colors, darkened glasses, a wedding band, obesity, and over-sized clothing.

Holding the hands together with the index fingers extended and touching (similar to a steeple) while the other fingers are wrapped together is appropriately called "steepling". This is a subliminal gesture which represents power, knowledge, and confidence. Unfortunately, it can also hint arrogance, pride, vanity, or a haughty attitude. Experts suggest you use steepling when you are in a meeting and want to make a point. Steepling might then imply that you are confident and knowledgeable about your subject. Open arms exhibit warmth, accessibility, approval, and love.

I'll never forget one time I met Kristin, my young granddaughter who was about three at the time, as she was coming off an airplane. She caught sight of me and began to run as fast as her little legs would carry her. I stooped down to greet her at eye level. In an instant, she tackled me so hard that we were both on the floor. Not a word was necessary. It was pure, unabashed acceptance and genuine love. We must have looked strange lying there on the airport floor hugging each other, but it is a memory I wouldn't want to trade. Wouldn't it be nice if everyone were as free as a little child to show love.

We all recognize the thumb under the chin with fingers resting on the cheek. This is the traditional thinker's position. There's the "okay" sign with the thumb and forefinger making a circle. When someone absorbs himself with an article such as glasses or his pen, he may be stalling for time. While hesitating, he might also push his chair back, cross his ankles, scratch his head, or narrow his eyes.

Hunching the shoulders implies a person is carrying a heavy load. A lowered head could mean modesty, reverence, or guilt. A hand to the chest conveys integrity, honesty, or amazement.

Handshakes determine the warmth of a relationship. Greater warmth is shown when one shakes the right hand and brings his left hand over their two entwined hands. Sometimes the forearm is grasped as well as the hand. And when even more warmth is intended, you'll see the left hand being put on the shoulder or even around the shoulder in a hug. We tend to respect and take more seriously a person who has a firm handshake. A whimpy handshake makes us doubt that person's warmth, honesty, and self-worth.

Erect posture speaks confidence and high self-esteem while slumped posture communicates low spirits, fatigue, or inferior feelings. Depressed people walk around with their head down, sometimes hands in their pockets. Muggers, when stalking victims, are aware of this head-down position assuming that person is more vulnerable, an easy target.

How we sit in a chair sends a message too. Balancing on the edge of a chair or playing with one's ring indicates nervousness or stress. Leaning back with both hands placed behind the neck suggests the person is feeling confident, dominant, even superior. Just leaning back in a chair might mean a person is at ease while leaning forward indicates interest.

I was watching Regis and Kathy Lee the other day, and several journalists were being interviewed. I couldn't help noticing how with one guest Kathy Lee just sat back in her chair and talked with her. But when the next journalist came out, she leaned forward in her chair and smiled freely showing genuine warmth and interest.

How often do we see someone shielding her mouth while talking to another? This may suggest the person is lying. Her hand creates an involuntary barrier for her untrue words. Experts say when we enter a room we should not shield ourselves behind a purse or brief case. They say carrying it at our side shows openness and warmth.

Scratching or pulling at the ear could mean the person is confused, wants to understand better, or has an itchy ear. Successful people have their share of stress. It can be recognized by rubbing the eyes or cheek, constantly repositioning oneself in a chair, and blinking frequently.

Smiling is such a simple gesture but it says so much. A genuine smile can lift the spirits, both of the sender and the receiver. But some smiles are not genuine. You can recognize an insincere smile because it never reaches the eyes. Smiles can send many messages: friendliness, happiness, politeness, or that you are trying to appease someone. Women smile more than men and appease more with smiles. Smiles are good, but they can work to our disadvantage if used too frequently and for the wrong reasons.

When we watch someone's face we can tell which emotion is being felt. By watching the rest of their body we can determine the intensity of that emotion. In conversations we tend to move our bodies toward the person we are interested in and away from those we are not.

Men and women differ some in body language. Women generally look at a person when they are *speaking* to them (seeking a reaction?) while men look at a person when they are *listening* to them. The more space a person takes, the more dominant he or she appears. Not only are men generally larger than women, they spread out their bodies more when they sit down. Sitting back in their chairs, legs are spread apart, or one leg is drawn up with the foot resting on the other knee. Arms are sometimes spread across the backs of chairs. On the other hand, women commonly sit with legs together and arms closer to the body. Should women try that masculine pose, no doubt they would appear threatening to the men in the room because it is not the usual female behavior. A woman often nods her head in conversation meaning "I hear what you are saying." When a man nods his head it probably means "I agree". Consequently, there can be some confusion when the two sexes communicate.

Women are more free with gestures than men. Gestures are okay if necessary to get your point across, but too many hand gestures discredit us. Those perceived as authoritative use fewer gestures. As in a golf swing, let your gestures follow through. Body language specialists say that short jerky gestures may cause one to believe your thoughts and words are also disconnected.

A person's eyes reveal more secrets than other body language. Eye-contact gains us respect and endorsement. In ordinary conversation people look at each other 30 to 60% of the time. For those intimately involved, the percentage is even greater. Direct eye-contact lasts between seven and 10 seconds. Longer looks might send an intimidating message and make the other person feel uncomfortable. Or it could suggest sexual interest. Our pupils automatically increase in size when we're attracted to someone or they to us. Other things can cause this, too. We tend to trust those whose eye-contact is direct, and we recognize warmth in them. Their undivided attention to our words builds our self-esteem. On the other hand, averted eyes suggest deceitfulness. Our eyes portray a range of emotions: love, hate, frustration, disgust, anger, exasperation, fear, compassion, charity, and surprise. If direct eye-contact is difficult, experts say "to focus on the nose or somewhere else on the face. They won't know the difference." they say.

The eye-level, too, is important. Kare Anderson in *Getting What You Want* says, "In a group the person with the highest eye-level is perceived as the leader. People tend to address that person first." Kare tells of a little 5'2" lawyer named Sarah who kept getting interrupted in meetings. At one particular meeting, though, just before she wanted to make an important point, she got up to get herself a cup of coffee. While still standing, thus having the highest eye-level, she raised her point. With everyone looking up at her, it was well received.

Even our clothes and our manner of speaking tell something about us. Wearing colorful clothing indicates we are people-oriented while conservative clothing says we are task-oriented. Speaking slowly and in lower tones makes us appear more believable. Slower speech denotes friendliness and contemplation, but sometimes boredom.

Another well-known and extremely effective tactic is to mirror another's body language. Successful people use it all the time. It sends the message that we have something in common and makes the other person feel comfortable with us. If they stand, we stand. If they sit we sit, If they cross their legs, so do we. If they finger their tie, we brush some lint off our blouse or shirt. We shouldn't be obvious, just allow a few seconds delay, then and do something similar to what they have just done. Some experts suggest using the opposite side. If he scratches his left shoulder, we rub our right shoulder. After a while, we can try "leading"--uncross our arms and see if the person follows our body language. If so, they have warmed up to us. Mirroring happens naturally with people who are attracted to each other.

So how can we use this knowledge of body language? We can use it to project a more professional image. Stand tall and sit tall, let our posture speak volumes. We can consciously control our body movements to enhance our effectiveness and credibility. We can monitor our speech patterns. We can use direct eye contact when talking or listening. We can give a firm handshake. We can dress the way we want to be perceived. When we enter a room we can make a good first impression. We can learn more about body language by turning down the volume on the TV set and studying the characters' movements. We can enlist a friend to watch our body language and help us recognize negatives. Then we can work on polishing our nonverbal actions.

Being more proficient in our "second" language will enhance all our relationships. It will help us better understand coworkers' sometimes indirect communication. When our nonverbal language is consistent with our words, we will we be sending out the messages we intend. And we will then be perceived as the professionals we really want to be--believable and credible.

(1) *Louder than Words: Nonverbal Communication* by A. Barbour
(2) (Other experts say study says 8-20%)
(3) Other material

CHAPTER 12

Goals are Dreams in Disguise

It's been a rough day. You've slaved hard setting goals for those under your authority. You've selected a long-term goal for each of them, and perhaps a short-term goal as a means of reaching that long-term goal. You feel good. You've made real progress. Good for them!

But what about your *own* life? Do you diligently slave over goals for your life the way you do for others? Or do you let life just happen? Sometimes we get so busy doing the best for our charges and our employers that we neglect the planning and development of our personal lives. If we learn to look at our lives as a whole, rather than just through the eyes of our job responsibilities, we'll be better managers of our time and subsequently feel less pressured. Goals help us to do this.

Many people shy away from setting goals. They spend more time planning a big party than their life. Only 3% of Americans put their goals in writing. They are generally high achievers. Those who neglect goal-setting may not fully understand its benefits.

My husband resists goal-setting. He's happy; he likes to laugh; he likes people; and he likes to let life unfold as it will. I, on the other hand, am a planner. I set goals and delight in meeting them. One time, he accompanied me on a speaking engagement. There he was finally challenged to re-think his stance on goal-setting. It wasn't necessarily what *I* said.

When I finished the morning segment just before lunch, Miss Indiana, Dayna Brewer, was introduced. She sang a couple songs and shared a few words. Without knowing in advance my subject was professionalism and goal-setting, Dayna told how she had achieved her long-time desire to be Miss Indiana. What touched my husband was her choice of words. She didn't talk about setting a goal and reaching it; she told of realizing a childhood *dream*--her *dream* of becoming Miss Indiana. Rick could better relate to the concept of dreaming. Somehow it seemed less threatening than goal-setting.

We all have hopes and dreams for ourselves and our families. We want to marry and have children. We want them to be successful. We want to own a home and establish strong friendships. We want to play the guitar and learn a foreign language. We want to go back to school and get a degree. We want to travel. We want to quit smoking. We want to begin an exercise program and lose weight. We want to do something meaningful with our lives.

Yet, few of us are disciplined enough to seriously pursue many of our goals. If you are prone to resist goal-setting, I'd like to challenge you to think of goal-setting as a means of fulfilling your "dreams."

Why would one want to set goals, anyway? Setting and achieving goals builds positive self-esteem within us. Self-esteem makes us feel good about ourselves thus we are happier and subsequently healthier. Focusing on goals for our future helps get us through difficult times right now. Goals, or dreams, help us live with integrity, to be true to ourselves. Once we establish specific standards of behavior that are right for us, our goals help us remain true to those standards. Goals also help us live with a purpose. They are like a road map. We wouldn't travel cross country without a map. Why then would we want to travel the road of life without direction? Goals allow *us* to determine what we want out of life and protects us from allowing others to maneuver us into *their* plan. When we set goals, our actions then can reflect those goals. For instance, if our goal is to pay off our new car quickly, our actions would be to think twice before squandering money on non-essentials.

So how do you go about setting goals for your life? How do you incorporate your goals into the many necessary daily activities that clutter your to-do list? First, determine what really matters in your life. Then write a life-time goal or a mission statement. To set that goal, ask yourself these questions: *What do I want my life to say? Who am I? Why am I here? Where am I going? What is absolutely most important in my life? What would I be willing to die for? After my death, how do I want to be remembered as a mom, daughter, son, employee, neighbor, friend or church member? If I achieve nothing else in life, I definitely want to...*" In other words, what characterizes your life? What really matters to you?

Perhaps your lifetime goal is to be a world traveler. How would you accomplish that goal? You would incorporate ways of working it into your lesser goals. You would learn all you could about the countries you wanted to visit. You would become proficient in several languages. You would investigate means of travel. You would work extra hard to save up money for the trips. You would seek ways to extend your vacation time.

So once that all important lifetime goal is determined, you then set long-term, mid-term and short-term goals, always keeping in mind your lifetime goal. Long-term goals generally project about two to five years into the future, mid-term a year, and short-term, a month. Men can more easily project five years into the future, but for us women, it's often difficult. Circumstances readily change in our lives. An unexpected pregnancy, a divorce, or a husband's job transfer could easily upset your five-year goals. These circumstances, though, need not disturb your life-time goal which is basically the mission statement for your life.

Though I have some long-term aspirations, both personal and professional, 1 devote more time to my mid-term and short-term goals. I like to begin each new year by setting yearly goals in several categories: personal, household, professional, financial, political, spiritual, social and health. You might choose other categories. (Please don't think I have it all together where goal-setting is concerned. I don't. I'm a long way from where I'd like to be. Yet I continue to press on, and eventually, I meet many of them. Here's an example, though not necessarily the real ones, of how I might write goals:

Personal: I will read at least one book a week this year. I will talk less and listen more. I will be more open-minded.

Household: I will have a six-month supply of food on hand for emergency purposes. I will replace the master bedroom wallpaper and dining room carpet.

Family: I will keep in touch with the kids by phoning, writing or e-mailing them each week. I will send letters and/or little gifts to the grandchildren each month. I will surprise Rick by planning three special getaway weekends this year. I will spend less time working nights when he is home. I will stop by and visit my mother or take her out weekly.

Professional: I will finish writing the book on professionalism. I will take five more speaking engagements this year. I will keep my office running smoothly by staying organized. I will do something every day to become better organized. I will keep in contact with people in my field by phone or by personal visits in order to remain aware of their needs, frustrations, successes, and ideas. I will locate three new distributors to market my products.

Financial: I will pay my house off by the end of this year. I will save $XXX monthly. I will balance my checking accounts each month when the statements arrive.

Political: I will write and call my congressman and stand up for causes I strongly believe in.

Spiritual: I will seek more fully to know God's will for my life. I will pray broader, putting others needs above my personal ones. I will utilize more fully my gift of encouraging others. I will memorize two scripture verses a month.

Health: I am keeping my fat intake under 20%. I will drink six glasses of water a day. I will be ten pounds lighter by January of next year. I will walk at least half an hour four times each week. I will have a physical exam complete with a treadmill stress test and a cholesterol test.

Social: I will get to know my neighbors better by inviting one family to dinner each month. I will work less and make time for fun with friends at least two times a month.

Notice all my goals are specific and measurable and are written in the positive, "I will" or "I am." I do not say I will *try to* finish writing my new book or invite my neighbors over. I say "I will." I have a lot of goals. Naturally, I can not work on all these goals at once so I might choose a couple to concentrate on each week. If I'm wise, I commit these two goals to 3 X 5 cards and keep them handy--on my bulletin board, on the bathroom mirror, in the car, or in my Bible. As I read my positive statement goals over each day, my mind begins to believe and act on what I am telling it. And it works!

It's so easy to fall in the trap of just planning day-to-day, making detailed to-do lists. These lists are very important, but they need not take priority over our goal plan. We must learn to merge the two together. Time Management expert Stephen Covey recommends that we plan *weekly*, not *daily*. He says scheduling day-by-day leads to a focus on urgency and a loss of perspective. He recommends we concern ourselves with people and relationships, not schedules. He encourages us to first review our life-time goal or mission statement. Then Covey suggests, before the week begins, that we ask ourselves what is the most important thing we can do in the upcoming week in regard to each of our roles in life: our profession, Mom, Dad, wife, daughter, son, church member, etc. Covey says before we commit anything else to our schedule, we should set aside time for each of these activities. That way, what's really important doesn't get neglected as we plan the many activities required to fulfill our busy schedules.

Many more would plan goals for themselves if they just knew how. It's not that difficult. (I believe it was Zig Ziglar who pointed out the following goal-planning method and a similar scenario.) Let's take again the supposed life-time goal of being a world traveler. Set your yearly goals (mid-term) which will reflect your life-time goal:

* I will take an extra job three nights a week this year to save for trips.
* I will carry my lunches four days a week rather than eating out to save money for traveling.
* This year I will read twelve books on countries I want to visit.
* I will take a course in Chinese at the local university.
* I will learn about European and Chinese cultures by talking with natives from those areas.

* I will work on my other goals also.

Now look over your upcoming month (short-term goal) and then plan your coming week. Try to work in activities that will further your goals.

* This week I will visit two travel agencies and discuss trips to China and to Rome.
* I will check my frequent flyer miles and see if they can be applied to an overseas trip.
* I will contact various airlines for routes and specials. I will talk with Chinese people about things to see in their country.
* I will look for a second job.
* I will work on my other goals also.

Finally, make your daily to-do list. Besides the many necessary tasks, be sure to add something each day that will help to further your goals:

Monday: I will call the Chinese club and set a date to meet with members and discuss their country.
Tuesday: I will pick up two travel books at the library.
Wednesday: I will contact the employment office about a part-time job.
Thursday and Friday: I will work on other goals.

Can you see how they all fit together? Your life is coming into balance. Things are starting to make sense. There's a master plan rather than just a lot of daily commotion.

You can use the same process with professional goals determining why you are in your profession. Develop a written mission statement. Decide what you want to accomplish in the coming year. Break those goals down into months and weeks, and finally put them on your to-do list.

You are in a challenging profession. It can totally consume your time and your energy leaving little else for your family and yourself. Sure, you want to be the best you can be. And you should be! But keep in mind that your career is only *part* of your life. You can treat your family (and yourself) to the best of you, too, by setting goals which include them. Goals bring out the best in you. They help you accomplish what's really important in life. And if you're still not convinced, well, think of goals as dreams, do a little planning, and then sit back and watch those dreams come true.

CHAPTER 13

Making Time Count

If there's one thing people are short of it's time! It seems wherever I go, the number one complaint is always the same-- *not enough time!*. Granted, we can't invent more time, but let's look at some ways to better utilize the time we do have.

First, we need to take charge of our time. Think of it like a budget. Look at each hour and each minute as a free gift placed in your account. You have so much money each month for food, clothing, recreation, etc. You learn to control your spending so you don't overspend. You wouldn't allow others to control your budget, so why your time?

Someone once said..."Failure to plan on your part does not constitute an emergency on my part."

To the compassionate-natured person who finds it hard to say no to anyone, this quote may appear harsh. There comes a time, though, when you're stretched to the limit and have to take an objective look at where your time is actually going. You might start by recording every 15-minute segment for two weeks just to find out how you are spending your time. Include not only work accomplished, but interruptions, phone calls, meetings, and planning time. Put the time beside each notation. When completed, look for a pattern of time wasters. Get rid of them as quickly as possible. Professionals are indeed active, but don't confuse that activity with productivity. You can spin your wheels all day and accomplish little. Like young mothers, professionals are faced with constant interruptions. Still, try to avoid running in all directions and leaving a job half done to start another one. Concentrate your efforts on things that offer the best long-term benefit.

Use a personal planning calendar (*Day-Timer**, *Day Runner,* and the *Franklin Planner* are good ones), and carefully plan each day. Statistics show that high achievers are generally planners and goal-setters. Many do their planning first thing in the morning. If that's your choice of time, grab yourself a cup of coffee and begin. Decide what you *have* to do, what you'd *like* to do, and what you *should* do. This sets priorities on your tasks. Generally expect things to take longer than you think. There's a tendency to over-plan. Don't. You'll end up frustrated because you can't accomplish it all. Schedule not just the time of those under your authority, but map out personal planning time, organizing time, cleaning time, and breaks. Allow a little cushion for unexpected happenings. Set deadlines, and promise yourself a reward when they're met--a coffee break, a shopping trip, or time to read your favorite business publication.

Identify your most productive time, often the first hour. Schedule your most challenging tasks then. Save easy jobs like opening mail for less productive times. With so many duties to accomplish, break duties down into the broadest possible categories--*needs, projects, outings, phone calls, clients, finances.* As you go through your day, regularly ask, "Am I spending my time wisely just now?" This helps to keep you on track."

Make use of small bits of time. In every 24 hour period, there are 96 fifteen-minute periods. If you are having trouble accomplishing a project, divide it up into 15-minute segments. Books have been written in 15 good minutes a day. It's been figured that one can read 15 books a year by devoting just 15 minutes a day to reading. You could sweep out your car in 15 minutes, or arrange your clothing in your closet.

Those segments of time add up. If you saved 30 seconds every five minutes, at the end of a day you'd have saved an hour. Do double duty by making use of otherwise wasted time. Keep a list of five-minute jobs near the phone. While on the phone, do one--clean a shelf, straighten a file drawer, clean or file your nails. Have five minutes before a meeting? Take inventory of supplies on hand, make a shopping list, or send an e-mail. Another idea is to save those piddling little jobs that mount up, and schedule a two-hour unpressured period each week to do them all.

Finally, schedule time for yourself. You're not being selfish when you do this; you're guarding yourself against burnout. You give so much and now it's your turn. Find a hermit spot and retreat there daily. This might be propped up on your bed savoring a good book, sitting under a shade tree sipping iced tea, curled up in an easy chair next to the fire, relaxing in a hot bubble bath, or walking in the woods. Wherever, sit back and relax for a few minutes. You deserve it!

Day-Timer will give you, just for writing or calling, a free 3-month starter planner calendar in a vinyl wallet complete with an address book. Their address is: One Day-Timer Plaza, Allentown, PA 18195-9986. Phone: 1-800-556-5430

CHAPTER 14

Points to Ponder on the Path to Professionalism

We sometimes get so busy with the day-to-day activities and responsibilities that we forget to reflect on our personal and professional growth. Well, maybe today's the day to do that. Why not grab yourself a cup of coffee or a cold drink, and I'll get my tea. Then let's sit back and together explore some professional pointers.

1) Conquer fear. Let's first look at an obstacle that hampers so many of us--*fear.* Is there something you'd really like to accomplish in life but are afraid you might fail? Does fear keep you from being all that you could be? I've heard it said that we should walk the middle ground between risk-taking and being too cautious. Caution is a good thing. Decisions definitely need to be made with circumspection, yet anybody who's ever been truly successful has, at some point, had to throw caution to the wind. I'm reminded of what the naval commander in the midst of war at sea said after reviewing his questionable odds. "Damn the torpedoes. Full speed ahead!"

After seriously weighing our options, unless we want to stay where we are and not grow or achieve much, there comes a time to take a leap of faith. It's obvious a chasm cannot be crossed in two leaps. It's all or nothing. But we wouldn't attempt leaping across that chasm unless we felt reasonably sure that we could make it. We prepare ourselves thoroughly and finally take the leap. And when we do, and find ourselves safely on the other side enjoying the fruits of our risk-taking, we wonder why we waited so long. If we're honest with ourselves, we'll recognize the culprit holding us back was most likely fear.

A University of Michigan study as quoted by Denis Waitley in *10 Secrets of Greatness* determined that 60% of our fears are totally unwarranted; 20% have already become past activities and are completely out of our control; and another 10% are so petty they don't really make any difference at all. Of the remaining 10% of our fears, only 4 to 5% are real and justifiable fears. And even of those, we couldn't do anything about half of them," says Waitley. "The final half or 2% of our fears which are real," he says, "we can solve easily if we stop stewing and start doing...knowledge and action."

We all have fears that plague us, but when we conquer them, our confidence is bolstered. We feel that we can tackle something more difficult. Years ago I had a fear about driving on interstates. Oh, it wasn't the fear of an accident, but the fear of getting lost (all interstates looked alike). I'd once heard the quote, "Do the thing you fear and you won't be afraid anymore." So I kept driving on the interstates. Year after year when several of us would go together to our state conventions in Indianapolis or elsewhere, I was always the one to drive. They didn't know how afraid I was. My husband would draw me detailed maps getting me through the city and showing me which exit and on ramp to take. I mean, just getting through the city of Indianapolis kept me praying earnestly. But the more I drove on interstates and through big cities, the more comfortable I became with them. Today, I don't think twice about tackling a highway trip. I've found that we don't have to let fear hold us in bondage. We can conquer our fears by facing up to them, by doing the thing we fear.

2) Take Responsibility for your own life. It's so easy to pass the blame. "I had a bad childhood." "I was born to a poor family." "My mother was a large woman so I'm predisposed to being heavy." "If my employer would just give me a decent budget, I wouldn't complain so much." Our happiness and satisfaction in life, as well as our success, demands that we quit blaming others and begin to take full responsibility for our lives and our actions.

Charles Givens in *SuperSelf* states, "To design and control your future effectively, you must first let go of your past. The more you dwell on the past, the more the past limits and controls your future. In taking control of your life, you must begin with a clean slate. That means dumping the garbage of the past and its hold on you," he says. This garbage could be a financial collapse, loss of a child or spouse, a bad relationship with a parent, or even child abuse. Givens recommends that we begin by accepting ourselves exactly as we are--in a broken relationship, in debt, in a wheelchair, in a fat body, in an non-fulfilling job, whatever. I love Givens saying, "Where I is, is where I is, but where I'm going is up to me." We can begin by keeping our eyes on the present. The past is behind us and no longer real. The only power it has over us is the power we give it.

3) Be a trouble-shooter. Trouble-shooting or problem-solving may fascinate you, or you may, like me, say, "No thank you. I am a creative person. Leave the problem-solving to those gifted in that area." I don't care *why* the car sounds funny, or what makes the air-conditioner run--just so it does. On the other hand, Rick makes his living solving other people's problems.

When we put up the Christmas tree last year, he fussed with a string of lights for an hour. I said, "The things are so cheap, why bother?" He said, "You don't understand how I think." He had to find *why* it didn't work. Still, no matter what our nature is in regard to problem-solving, there are times we all have to do it. So we may as well learn how.

The first step is to stop and think before we speak. Stephanie Culp in *You Can Find More Time For Yourself Every Day* encourages us, "Be a trouble-shooter. When you run into a problem, try to think of at least two solutions before you take it to your boss." In doing so, we may well come up with a solution before we bother him (or her). At the least, our boss will know that we have given the matter serious thought.

Here are a few techniques professional trouble-shooters use. They can well be applied to our profession. First, overlook what's *not* working, and look at the entire situation. Try to analyze how it works normally and how the problem affects the whole picture.

Next, see if the problem is caused by something other than the obvious because you may be looking at the effect and not the cause. Ask the person bringing the problem to you to please explain it fully. In doing so, he or she may come to understand the problem better and possibly come up with their own solution.

And if you still don't get it, say "I don't understand the problem the way you are explaining it to me. Could you tell me in a different way?" By stepping back and talking it over with them, the problem may be solved quickly and agreeably. And by using trouble-shooting tips like these, you may well prevent broken relationships and save yourself much undo frustration.

4) Put a price on your time. It's easy to fall into the trap of "doing it all." But we need to ask ourselves, "How much is my time worth?" Ruth Klein in *Women as Managers* suggests we determine if spending $7 an hour for a courier is wiser than driving the distance to the post office ourselves. She says we need to ask ourselves if we can accomplish more than $7 worth of work in the time we've saved? Successful people don't do what they can get someone else to do for them. You may need something from *Walmart* and plan to run out after the morning's activities. But if you have a subordinate or a volunteer coming right past the store on her way in, why not ask her to pick up the needed items. You can spend your time more productively. Also, by planning your days, weeks, and months carefully, you, not circumstances, are in control of your time and consequently your life.

5) Choose your words carefully. Our words label us. There are over 450,000 words in an unabridged English language dictionary. Surprisingly, though, most people use only about 400 of them in 80% of their everyday conversation. Denis Waitley (in the above mentioned book) recommends reading as one way to increase our word power. He notes that "only 5% of people living in the United States will either buy or read a book this year." Successful people read. The library is a great place to frequent.

Like other successful people, we need to speak positively and eliminate negative talk. We might say, "I'm very pleased." not "I couldn't be more delighted." Or, "I know you're busy, so I'll be on my way." rather than "l won't bug you any longer." Also we need to be cautious of comfortable phrases we often speak. Phyllis Mindell in *A Woman's Guide to the Language of Success* reminds us to avoid preceding statements with words like "I think." or "I guess." She says these statements label us as indecisive. Stephen Coscia in *Customer Service Over the Phone* suggests we change our "you" statements to "I" statements. Rather than say, "*You're* confusing me." say, *"I'm* confused." Instead of "What did you say?" *try* "I'm sorry, I didn't hear your last sentence."

6) Focus. Successful people determine where they are headed by setting goals. Then they "focus" on those goals and objectives. Focus involves disciplining our minds; concentrating our energy on the appointed tasks as if they are the only things that matters. *Focus* is just a little word but it says so much. Especially as professionals, when our minds and bodies are pulled in so many directions at once, we must learn to focus. Personally, it's a priceless word which I use regularly to keep myself on track. In my business there are so many opportunities to write in different genres, to become involved in similar work, and to take on new products and business ventures. So I must continually remind myself "Focus!" "Focus on your goals and focus on your responsibilities." If I try to branch out in too many different directions I become ineffective in the things I have set out to do.

7) See yourself a winner. Be a visionary. Decide where you want to go and actually see yourself there and doing the things you hope to achieve. Dwell on that picture often. Dream big. Don't limit yourself. Negative thoughts will come both from others and from within. Put them away quickly. Replace them with a pre-planned positive statement: "I am really great at putting on large community events."or "I am very comfortable with public speaking." or "It's wonderful finally having that degree in hand." Confess the answer as if it has already been achieved. Les Giblin in *How to Have Confidence and Power in Dealing with People* says, "Act as if you believe in yourself and others will believe in you."

8) Believe the truth about yourself. How often are we devastated when we hear that someone has spoken negatively about us? Perhaps it's the way we talk, walk, sing, dress, work, eat, whatever. If we are not careful, we begin to believe those lies about us. We need to ask ourselves, "What makes their opinion any better than our own?" We need to start with the premise that we are each unique individuals. We do not have to think, speak or act to fit anyone else's mold. We get into trouble when we value the criticizer's opinion more highly than we do our own. We need to trust our own judgement.

As a schoolboy, Thomas Edison was sent home with a note from his teacher saying that he could not learn, that he could not think, that he was stupid. If Edison had believed those lies, we might still be using candles instead of enjoying the benefits of electricity.

9) Treat others the way you want to be treated. Treat everyone you meet as if they are the most important person you will meet that day. Look them directly in the eye and really listen when they talk. Les Giblin in his book (mentioned above) relates this story: Walt Whitman and a friend were walking down the street. Whitman stopped and engaged a stranger in conversation. For 15 or 20 minutes Whitman monopolized the conversation and the other fellow hardly got a word in. When the stranger left, Whitman turned to his friend and said, "Now there's an intelligent man!" He had been kind to hear Whitman out. Whitman was pleased and satisfied.

Everyone has a need for appreciation. When you appreciate another, you affirm their personal worth. When you approve others, it reflects back on you. Giblin also says, "Look for something to approve in the other person. It may be something small or insignificant. But let the other person know you approve *that*, and the number of things you can sincerely approve of will begin to grow." He goes on to say, "When the other person gets a taste of your genuine approval, he will begin to change his behavior so that he will be approved for other things." Give appreciation and you will receive appreciation. Give kindness and it will come back to you. Give understanding, and you'll receive understanding. Be thoughtful, and others will treat you more thoughtfully.

10) Be enthusiastic. Successful people create excitement and enthusiasm about what they do. *What is enthusiasm?* The thesaurus describes it as "ardor, zeal, fire, anticipation, eagerness." The dictionary says "intense or eager interest." We need to think big--to look for contagious ideas that will excite coworkers and those under our care, and even the community. When I was a professional director in a long-term care center, enthusiasm came naturally to me. There was no need to *create* excitement about my work; it spilled over to anyone who would listen. I've heard those who love their job say things like, "Sometimes I feel guilty taking money for this job." or "I would work this job even if thy didn't pay me." If that's not enthusiasm about what they do, I don't know what is.

Well, there you have ten key points to pursue on the path to professionalism. There are so many more. You've come a long way already, and may even have an impressive title. But a title alone does not make one successful or professional. It's growing and learning. It's that day to day struggle to be all that you can be. It's actively pursuing points like the above. So keep up the good work.

CHAPTER 15

Coping With Criticism Constructively

Suppose, for a moment, that you work at a health care center like I once did. It's Friday morning. It's been a hectic week at work. Your assistant is home sick. The state surveyors are due any time, and you're pushing to have everything in order. You're responsible for a big company event tonight, and you have a care-plan meeting in 15 minutes. You've just finished morning rounds and you're rushing to your office to jot some last minute notes. On the way, you must pass the break room. As you come closer, you stop dead in your tracks. Gossip!

"She sure has it made! What an easy job! She doesn't punch a time clock. She just jumps in the van and goes anytime she wants. Oh sure, she takes a resident or two, but who knows where she goes or what she does? And look how nice she dresses? She probably makes a bundle. Why doesn't she have to wear a uniform like us? She doesn't spend *that* much time with residents! She's always in her office doing who knows what!"

You push back a tear as the cutting words wound your very spirit. You know they are talking about you. Then anger takes over. Your first impulse is to march in there and give them an earful.

How dare they criticize you when you know you probably work circles around all of them! After all, you don't have time to take a break--and gossip! But then you think better of it. You turn, unseen, and walk back to your office. But your day is ruined!

Or is it? It doesn't have to be. We can choose several responses when criticism is thrust upon us. We can become angry, hurt, bitter, resentful, or self-righteous. We can withdraw and ignore them all. We can burn ourselves out trying to live up to our criticizer's expectations. We can become hardened, or we can become compassionate and forgiving.

Realize that no matter where you go in life, or what you do, you can always expect complaints--or find yourself in the position of having to issue them. Rejection is a difficult thing for us all, and when someone complains about us or our work, we feel the sting sharply. For us, it probably hurts even more since we go to such great lengths to please everyone. If you have passed that magical two-year testing period where you either quit, or begin your training as a seasoned professional, you have probably learned to toughen up a bit where thoughtless criticism is concerned. Still, none of us are immune to the pain. And being aware of that pain, we are better able to consider the feelings of others when we must issue a complaint against them.

It's been said, "There is a hint of truth in all criticism." An old proverb says, "A rebuke goes deeper into one who has understanding than a hundred blows into a fool." If we can learn from the criticism, we're one step ahead of the game. Recently I was challenged to do just that.

I am a friendly person. I like people, and I like to see to their comfort whether they are guests in my home, or elsewhere. Recently I was at a monthly dinner meeting that I attend regularly. An old man appeared in the food line behind me. Since he was a first-time visitor, I introduced myself and said, "Here, go ahead of me, you're new here." He said, "You don't have to do that." But I really wanted to extend him an honor so I said, "Please, go before me." He did, but later in the evening, in a joking sort of way he told me I was pushy. I had never thought of myself that way before, but I took note. I will be more careful in the future. The good intentions of my heart may not have been perceived in the way they were meant.

Criticism comes in many ways. Perhaps a man comments on your modern new hair cut. You smile, pleased that he noticed. Then he spoils it by rudely adding, "It doesn't look good on you, though." What do you do? You can become defensive, informing your criticizer how much you paid for it and that you like it whether he does or not. Or you can hold back your anger and probe into his thinking process trying to locate the root of his comment. Ask questions. "Why did you say that? What style would you recommend? Why?" Perhaps the criticizer is an expert hair stylist. If you can look beyond the momentary criticism to the reason behind it, you may gain some costly information free.

Another trick when dealing with complainers is to agree with them. This defuses them quickly. Though they may be dead wrong in their complaint, find some little thing on which you can agree. "You're right! It has been a tough day! I agree with you." or "You're absolutely right I *have* been a grouch lately. Thank you for making me aware of it. I've been so busy getting ready for this state inspection and the party tonight that I haven't taken time to relax and smell the roses." Instead of having a war on your hands, you've probably made a friend.

When you've made a mistake, admit it quickly and emphatically. "I shouldn't have said that. It was inconsiderate of me. It must have made you feel badly. Please forgive me." An apology works so much better than sweeping it under the rug and hoping it will go away.

Recently I was having some printing done and I wrote a $2500 check to a printer. Several weeks later the contact person called me and asked if I had sent a check with the order. I assured her that I had and gave her the check number and the date it was written. She said she remembered receiving it and even recorded it in her book, but the check was not to be found. Rather than making excuses, she immediately admitted, "I take full responsibility. I am really sorry. I try to be neat, but my desk is just not like it should be. It could be in a drawer or I may have even thrown it in the trash. I'm really sorry for my carelessness! I will pay to have a stop payment put on it." Though it was a careless way to do business, the lady impressed me. I said, "I can see you are a very honest person. I admire that in you. I will write you another check." It took a big person to admit that she had personally failed--especially when it could have cost her her job. She had my respect.

Humor can defuse criticism and anger. If someone tells you your dog is the ugliest dog they've ever seen, tell them it's not a dog; it's an alligator. You will knock them off guard, and you can both have a good laugh with the critical comment forgotten. We mentioned this before, but it bears repeating. When a critical remark is made to your face, disarm the offender by asking him or her to repeat it. "Excuse me, I didn't catch what you said." This gives the criticizer a chance to reconsider a careless statement. If it is repeated at all, it will no doubt be kinder. And the criticizer will be more careful the next time he or she complains to you.

Before you respond to a criticism, look beyond your hurt emotions to discover the complainer's feelings behind their remark. Acknowledge them. "I understand this is a very embarrassing situation for you." Also look for their need behind their complaint and seek to meet it. The complainer may have a need to be recognized or to feel important. If you can still your own wounded pride to better understand their remark, some of the sting will be eased. When you do respond, try to sandwich your defense between compliments. It takes a big person to do this, but then directors are very unique individuals.

Take the scenario we started with. If you are confronted about how your job is an easy one, you might say something like this: "You know I really understand how you feel (acknowledge their feelings). I thought that, too, before I took this job. My job must appear quite glamorous. Many people think that (agree with them). But there is a down side, too. Your job is so important because you must care for the residents' physical needs. I'm so glad you are here for them. Not everyone could do what you do. Imagine how helpless the residents would be without your loving care! I'm sure *I* couldn't handle your job (compliment them)."

"Now let's look at my job. Rather than just meeting their physical needs, I must meet their emotional and recreational needs. Though it's different than your job, it's equally important. I would love to be with the residents all day long, but unfortunately my job responsibilities are regulated, and I must spend time doing paperwork, too. Though my job *looks* glamorous, it really can be grueling at times. Yes, I do get to wear pretty clothes, and it is nice to have the freedom to get out of the building occasionally (agree with them again), but with all freedom comes responsibility." Then explain your responsibilities. Share the duties of an outing, of hosting an activity, of paperwork, of evening responsibilities, and of not being able to go home just because the clock says it's time (defense). Finally, close with another compliment. "Thanks again for all you do for the residents, I really appreciate your effort (compliment)."

This may help them to understand your job or a particular problem, but know there are always some who will complain, just for the sake of complaining. No amount of reasoning will change their behavior. Realize it's probably not you personally they are criticizing; they are simply directing their own frustrations toward you. Hard as it is, try to show them kindness in spite of their actions. A soft answer turns away anger.

If your boss is critical of you, set your feelings aside for the moment. Ask him how *he* would have handled the situation. This keeps the criticism on the problem, not you. It lets him know you value his opinion, and it makes him think more seriously about the problem you have faced. Hopefully, he'll be more empathetic. The question might stir greater cooperation from him, and perhaps he'll even come up with a more workable solution.

When you must criticize someone, do so in private. Smile, even if you don't feel like it. Begin with agreement. As we said before, find something, no matter how small, on which you can agree. Again, sandwich the complaint between compliments.

Michael Thomsett in his book *Little Black Book of Business Etiquette* tells us: "Replace negative statements like, "Why can't you...?" or "I hate it when..." with positive statements like, "What if we...." or "Wouldn't it be better if..." Other experts encourage us to use lots of "I's" and not many "you's." *You's* can make a person feel criticized. Direct your criticism at the problem, not the person. "If you come to an impasse, stop and set new ground rules," says the Alexander Hamilton Institute in their publication, *How To Improve Your Negotiation Skills.* "Neither person may say anything until he has stated the opponent's view to the opponent's satisfaction."

It's never easy to face criticism, and it can be very unpleasant when you must give it. Still, if you stop and weigh your words carefully, you can avert some problems and settle others in a civil manner.

Another proverb says: "He who restrains his words has knowledge, and he who has a cool spirit is a man of understanding. Even a fool, when he keeps silent, is considered wise; when he closes his lips he is counted prudent." Once you lose your cool and raise your voice, the other person has the upper hand. Thomas Jefferson said it so well:

"Nothing gives one person so much advantage over another as to remain cool and unruffled under all circumstances." Sure, criticism will come and there will be tough situations to face, but be assured you can handle it. After all, God didn't give you broad shoulders for nothing.

CHAPTER 16

Clutter, Confusion, and Chaos

"Somebody help! My life is out of control!" If you are like the rest of us, occasionally you find yourself feeling overwhelmed by it all--so many decisions, so many choices, so many demands, so many responsibilities--and so little time. Then you are overtaken by unwanted clutter, confusion, and sometimes chaos. Oh, for a while you ride the wave, so to speak. You may even thrive on all the activity. But then one day the blinders fall and you shriek, "My life is a mess! I've got to do something."

Maybe you are one of the 16-million women with children under 18 who are holding down a full-time job--or a working father who is active in the kids' lives. Even if you are single, or your children are already reared, there are still too many things to be done, and not enough time or energy to do them. It seems like the more money we make, the more things we buy, and then the more time it takes to care for those things. It can be a vicious circle.

David Sharp in a terrific article, "So Many Lists, So Little Time," in *USA Weekend* (March 15-17, 1996) describes our situation pretty well: "These days speed is of the essence; anything that can't keep up becomes the cultural equivalent of roadkill. All the elements that represented life at its most leisurely in earlier eras-- picnic tables, porch swings, letter-writing--have given way to the manic pace of fast-food, drive throughs, computer games and e-mail. The overstuffed "in" box that sits on our desk or blinks in the corner of our laptop screens isn't just a sign of how backlogged our schedules have become--it's a symbol of our overloaded lives."

Sharp quotes Marcia Lasswell, an Los Angeles based therapist and president of *The American Association of Marriage and Family Therapists:* "The standards we've set for ourselves are based on the traditional family model from the 1950's and 1960's, when the husband supported the family and the wife had to look after the home and get involved in community and school activities. Women, in particular, have never given up that model."

"Stress-related illnesses cost the nation $300 billion a year in medical costs and lost productivity," says Sharp. He adds that "In the last five years, 28% of Americans voluntarily made changes that led to less income, but a more balanced life."

Unfortunately, as professionals, we are not immune to the stress and chaos that plagues the rest of the country. So we, like them, have got to find ways to bring some order back into our lives, to make them less stressful and more enjoyable. Let's explore some things that might help.

1) Scrutinize the situation. Take a good hard look at where you are. Are you happy there? What would be your ideal lifestyle? What changes can you make to bring your present lifestyle nearer to your ideal?

2) Identify what's important. As we discussed in chapter 11, set goals for yourself. Take time to think seriously about where you are going? Give yourself a seriously thought-out goal plan for your life?

Time management expert, Stephen R. Covey says in *Bottom Line Personal*, "We cannot identify what is truly important unless we step back and think at length about our daily routines. Only after considering what life is really all about will you be able to set priorities skillfully." He recommends that to determine which roles and values are most important to you, that you visualize your 80th birthday celebrating with family, friends, and business associates. What would you like them to say about your achievements--as a spouse, parent, neighbor, teacher and manager? Write down the comments you would like to hear. Covey says, "This exercise helps you prepare a personal mission statement which summarizes the values and lifetime goals to which you aspire. With this done," he continues, "you are ready to plan your time. Your objective is to balance your activities so that you can devote adequate time to advancing toward your personal goals in each of your roles."

3) Establish an "everything" book and carry it with you everywhere. It can be a commercial organizer, or just a 3-ring binder filled with paper and your calendars--weekly, monthly, and yearly. Whatever, this book is so much more than a calendar; it is your life in a book. Do you ever find yourself asking:

* Where did I write that number?
* What is the name of that gal I met at the spring workshop?
* If I could just remember that joke!
* What did my spouse ask me to pick up on the way home?
* What size shoes does Tommy wear?
* What is the color of my favorite lipstick?
* What was my New Year's resolution?
* When is Aunt Mary's birthday?
* What's the name of that bed and breakfast Mary told me about? What was the title of that book?
* What was my starting milage?
* What did I spend on groceries last month?

You get the idea. You also keep your goals and your dreams written in it and, most importantly, your master list.

4) Remember the master list where you keep track of everything to be done, both on the job and in your personal life. Once it is on paper, you don't have to clutter your mind remembering it.

5) Get your finances in order. It doesn't matter whether you make a lot or barely get by, you can still be in control of your finances. With easy credit and so many buying temptations, reckless spending is running rampant. Thomas Stanley and William Danko, in their best seller, *The Millionaire Next Door* subtitled "The Surprising Secrets of American's Wealthy" write that 62.4% of millionaires know exactly how much they spend each year for food, clothing, and shelter. In comparison, only

35% of high-income producing non-millionaires know. And how about the rest of us? Are we in control of our spending, or does it control us? Establishing a budget helps keep us on track. It allows us to plan ahead as to how we will spend, save, and give. If we don't already, we can save our receipts in a monthly expandable file folder and tally up totals each month. Then we can record them on a column analysis pad. That way, at a glance, we can see at the end of the year exactly where our money has gone.

6) Establish a regular planning time. I like to do this on Sunday evenings with a new week's calendar spread before me. When you plan, focus on relationships before schedules. Also, allow yourself some creative time to dream of what you'd like to be, do, and accomplish.

7) Establish a quiet time. A man told me of seeing a girl from his office at lunchtime sitting alone at a picnic table outside the building with her Bible open before her. She told him, since she wasn't a morning person, she was having her "quiet time" during her lunch hour. Quiet times can be used to pray, think, read, or plan.

You may want to take a breather, occasionally, from the daily pressures of your job. You might eat your lunch at a nearby park while you watch the squirrels play, or you might sit in your car and flip through a new magazine.

8) Forget perfectionism. Often, perhaps because of the way we were raised, or because of some driving force within us to perform, we push ourselves to do everything 100%. And that's just unrealistic. We are imperfect people. Once my daughter quoted me the old proverb, "If it is worth doing, it is worth doing well." I told her not all things required perfectionism. Sometimes it is better to "get the top layer off," so to speak, than to avoid tackling a job because you can't finish it perfectly.

9) Get the clutter out of your life. Look at your office and your home through new eyes, as someone else might see it. Has clutter slipped in unaware? Ask yourself, "What can I live without?" Go through closets and get rid of things that you don't wear. Check knick-knacks about the house. Are there too many? How about the refrigerator door? your desk drawer? the garage? Have a garage sale, or give away extras that clutter up your life. Use your waste basket freely.

10) Quit spending time doing things you don't really want to do. If you keep putting off some task, maybe your heart isn't really in it. Forget it, or delegate it.

11) Take care of yourself. When things get out of control, we don't always eat right, but just grab what's quick. Plan ahead what foods you will eat: fruits, vegetables, dairy products, and whole grains. Exercise, too, is a great stress reliever. We are often "too busy," but it pays big dividends in providing extra energy to complete our tasks.

12) Plan ahead. Plan menus for two weeks in advance, and shop for many things at once. Buy gifts in advance when you find them on sale. Give gift certificates or magazine subscriptions. Fill the car with gas at low-pressured times. Have extra keys made and keep them accessible. My daughter, Toni, who lives in Florida, recently had a weird key situation:

She arrived home, parked her car in her unattached garage, took her one and two-year-old children into the house, gave the baby her keys to entertain herself, and went back to get the groceries out of the car. When finished, she slammed the trunk, and ugh! She had caught her finger inside the closed lid. Now what! The babies were in the house--with the keys! Inside the garage with the overhead door closed, no one would have heard her yell. Desperate, Toni first prayed, and then she reached into the pocket of her husband's jacket that she was wearing. Low and behold, there were his keys. But having a Honda, with the key hole on the far right side, and her finger caught in the far left side, it took some gymnastics to unlock the trunk--but her unattended babies inside motivated her on. Thank goodness, she found the extra keys and eventually maneuvered the key into the lock and got free.

So *you* don't get locked out, plan ahead and store an extra key somewhere outside, like in a shed, that requires a combination lock to get into. This prevents an intruder from having access to a key stored outside the house.

13) Avoid interrupting yourself. Think twice before giving in to the urge to take a break from what you are working on. You may be versatile people who also like to move; sitting still is sometimes a chore. Consequently any opportunity to get up and do something else is coveted. Discipline yourself with the prospect of a reward: *If I work on this for five, 10, 15, or more minutes, I can take a walk.*

14) Read while you drive. Your library has novels on tape. A man who travels widely for S&S Worldwide told me that he "reads" five novels a week this way.

15) Other things you can do: Shop by phone or on-line. Order by catalog. Take advantage of businesses that deliver such as dry cleaners, copy shops, and pharmacies. Pay bills by mail. Send letters via e-mail. To avoid trips to the bank, consider direct-deposit. Turn off the TV and put on some peppy classical music to motivate you to get your chores done quickly.

Keep a list of frequently called numbers posted near the phone. Use a cordless phone so you can do two things at once. You don't have to answer the phone just because it rings. Let the answering machine get it and call back at your convenience. Get organized. Store things together that go together (I put coffee filters in the top of the coffee canister and the roll of garbage bags in the bottom of the wastebasket). Use plastic baskets to organize small things on the pantry shelf. Do the most difficult tasks first each day. The rest will be downhill. Keep a mini-tape recorder in the car for to-do's and for neat ideas that come to you while driving, or attach a note pad to your dashboard.

16) Relax and do nothing occasionally. As successful people, I know this is difficult to do, but life is too short just to work all the time. As the old saying goes, "Don't forget to smell the flowers."

Life can indeed be overwhelming at times, but hang in there. Remember you don't have to be all things to all people; just be true to yourself. Keep striving to alleviate the clutter, to avoid the unnecessary, and to take time for yourself and those you care about. After all, stress is just a little six-letter-word. You are a professional, and I know you can handle most anything--even stress.

CHAPTER 17

Friendship: A Present You Give Yourself

Oh how I wish I could sit down with each one of you, share a cup of tea, and have an intimate chat about the meaning of friendship. We would share about our many friends: childhood friends, current friends, and past friends. We'd discuss how we have been hurt by friends and how, in difficult times, we have been comforted by them. We'd talk about building new friendships and about keeping old ones in good repair. Oh we'd have a good time! I feel like we are already friends.

We all need to have good friends, at the very least, one special friend. Our professions are demanding, often without immediate tangible rewards. Frequently coworkers do not appreciate the magnitude of our responsibilities. They think we have the "easy" job. Subsequently, needed strokes from them are not always forthcoming.

That is where friends come in. They care about us. They rejoice when we pull off a successful event (they may even help). They care when we hurt. They are willing to be a sounding board when the tensions mount. We all need friends. As someone once said, "A friend is a present you give yourself."

Webster defines a friend as "a person one knows well and is fond of; an ally, supporter, or sympathizer." Somehow that seems so inadequate. You may have heard this definition: "Your friend is the man who knows all about you and still likes you." But I love this one even better: "One heart living in two bodies."

Friendship can be a fragile thing. It comes at a price. It needs regular maintenance just to survive. Friendship demands loyalty. If we can't trust our friends, who can we trust? When we open our hearts to embrace a friendship, we take on certain responsibilities. We will be there when that friend needs us, convenient or not. We will be genuine and honest, and we will remember, "Truth without love is cruel."

George Jean Nathan, in 1925, made an interesting yet confusing statement: "Love demands infinitely less than friendship." It may speak differently to you, but I think it is saying that friendship demands that you must work even harder to keep it alive than a love relationship. Perhaps the ideal situation is to combine the two. It has been said, "The best of lovers were friends before they were lovers."

One might think of friendship as a checking account. Money must be deposited if you wish to write checks (make withdrawals). The more checks you write, the more you must deposit. Likewise, for a friendship to continue, it must be a mutual thing. One person can't do all the taking, nor can he or she do all the giving.

Friends lovingly do for one another because they care about each other.

There are levels of friendship and qualities of friendship. The one quality I value most in a friend is trust. Some friends, I can be more open with than others. Within the precious inner circle, I can share my deepest hurt, my greatest ambition, or my most wicked thought, and know that I will not be condemned. I also know it will go no further. Though I love all my friends, I know there are some I would not open my heart to so freely.

True friendship knows no time limit. You can be apart a long time, and then, when you are together, it is like you've never been apart. "He who finds a friend finds a treasure." Other friendships are more shallow and cannot take the strain of separation. Today, with people moving so frequently, friendships can be quickly forgotten. Both parties may desire to continue the camaraderie, but eventually they drift apart.

Then there are a few people who want only one friend at a time. They are either your friend, or your enemy. When they are your friend, they want all of your time and devotion. When they are not, they don't have the time of day for you. Lavater said, "Be not the fourth friend of him who had three before and lost them."

"Choose your friends carefully. They tend to influence you for good or bad. They can affect how you dress, where you eat, your thoughts, and even your values. One friend at a Christian's women's group I attend always blesses me. She is so enthusiastic, and her vibrant faith just overflows to everyone she meets. She challenges me to keep on growing spiritually. There are many kinds of friends: childhood, adult, non-peer friends, couple friends, opposite-sex friends, married "best friends," heart friends, and casual friends. Some even have warm loving friendships with their pets. Others fall in love with their vehicle, clothes, and, unfortunately, even alcohol.

Probably the best way to describe friendship is to see it in action. Last year my youngest daughter, Toni, pregnant with her second child, went into labor at just five month. The doctors gave her no hope of a living baby. Still, they put her to bed and monitored her closely. Living in Florida, she was too far away for me (in Indiana) to help readily. *Enter friend Michelle:* Michelle, who lived four hours away from Toni, was fearful of highway driving. Still, her friend needed her. She kissed her beloved husband goodbye, packed up her young baby, and drove across the state to Toni's. Michelle was (and is) selfless. Monday through Friday, she would care for both their babies, cook, clean, and meet Toni's needs. On weekends, with Toni's husband home, Michelle would head back home. On Monday morning, though, she would return. This went on until Toni was able to get a live-in lady to help.

Thanks to the Good Lord, Michelle, and other friends, Toni at eight months into her pregnancy, gave birth to Kaity, our miracle baby. She was a perfect, beautiful, healthy baby girl with a full head of snow-white hair. Two-years-old now, and a bundle of energy, she's the delight of our lives.

Here's another example of friendship. As teens, my oldest daughter, Lisa, learned that her friend, Lori, was facing a problem. Lisa went to Lori's house when she wasn't home. Her mother let Lisa into Lori's room. There Lisa hid little uplifting scripture verses all over Lori's room. Lori told Lisa that she was finding them for a long time to come.

Some ten years and eight children (between them) later, *Lisa* found herself facing an extremely perplexing situation. After 12 years of what she thought was a happy and solid marriage and family life, it abruptly ended. Lisa was utterly devastated.

Lori, though she seldom wrote letters being so busy with her large family, wrote this to Lisa: "I can't be there to hide scripture verses around your house, but I will remember in my own way." Every week, thereafter, as long as it was needed, a handwritten encouraging note arrived from Lori, complete with comforting scripture verses.

Friendship knows no age limit. Wilma, at 92, is a good friend even though there is a 38 year difference in our ages. On the contrary, Rick and I have celebrated our 36th wedding anniversary, yet we have "couple friends" who are 30 years our junior. When hearts connect, age doesn't matter. And if you've read much of my work, you have probably guessed that Rick is my very "best" friend. His love and friendship toward me is best summed up in this quote: "What I cannot love, I overlook." And he overlooks much.

Another friendship I've always been in awe of is that of Toni and Mike. They became friends early; Mike was four, Toni five. They flew kites together, played baseball and broke out a church window together, made candy together, shopped together, and went on family vacations together. As teenagers the friendship grew. I'm just now hearing all the things they did back then that they shouldn't have--toilet papering their youth pastor's home regularly; gathering real estate signs from yards, and late one night, plunking them all down in someone special's yard; and driving around town and country while one of them was blindfolded in the passenger's seat. Meanwhile the other tried to get them lost. Then they switched seats and the rider had to find the way home.

Oh, there was nothing sexual in the relationship. Once when Toni lacked a date for a dance, as a last resort, she broke down and asked Mike to take her. Mike's response? "Yuk!" (And people regularly remark that Toni is a stunningly beautiful girl.)

When Toni was engaged, her very exceptional fiance, understanding she and Mike's unique brother/sister-like friendship, gave her permission to go to Florida with Mike--for one last spree. Today they are adults. Toni's married; Mike's not. When she comes home from Florida, she and Mike still get together (with her husband's permission, of course). She tries to train "bachelor" Mike in holding the children, assuring him they won't break.

Toni says, "We know *everything* about each other, and we still like each other. We have nothing in common anymore, but we still have fun together."

Back in 1931, Willa Cather said, "Only solitary men know the full joys of friendship. Others have their family, but to a solitary, and an exile, his friends are everything." My precious friend, Theresa, who came over from Scotland, doesn't have parents or sisters and brothers in this country. But there never was a more loyal friend. She treats all her friends as if they were family.

Some cherished childhood friendships continue into adulthood. My middle daughter, April, is an air-traffic controller at the Miami Regional Center in Florida. When she comes home she makes it a regular practice to get together with three or four friends from her grade school years. Though they've all grown up and have children now, they still enjoy each other's company.

Friendships need to be entered into cautiously. Fuller said "Let friendship creep gently to a height; if it rushes to it, it may soon run itself out of breath." Likewise, the character, Mary Richards, on the old Mary Tyler Moore show said, "Sometimes you have to get to know someone really well to realize you're really strangers."

But sometimes friendships fail. Perhaps it's because we expect perfection from our friends. Cyrus expressed it pretty well, "All men have their frailties; and whoever looks for a friend without imperfections will never find what he seeks. We love ourselves not withstanding, our faults, and we ought to love our friends in like manner."

But maybe that struggling friendship doesn't have to fail. Generally, it's a misunderstanding. Often someone has overstepped their boundaries by giving unwanted advice. You have to be very careful not to say anything negative about a friend's (even a best friend's) offspring. She (or he) may tell you how badly *their* kids are behaving, but be careful about agreeing with her or offering unsolicited advice. Generally, your female friend wants two things: a sympathetic ear, and for you to help her sort out her thoughts.

To mend a broken relationship, forgiveness is generally required. And it doesn't necessarily have to be initiated by the offender. It takes a big person to step forward, when he or she has been the wounded party, and seek to restore the friendship. But if this person wants the friendship badly enough, he or she might think of some way *they* have contributed to the breakup and apologize for that--perhaps a wrong attitude. This gives the offender a chance to save face and hopefully to apologize also. Sometimes it just takes time for a wound to heal.

My daughter, April, makes intense friendships, but when those friendships are so close, they sometimes fail. She told about a girl she works with. About four years ago they had a falling-out. Later April tried to bring healing to the relationship. The girl flatly refused. Then, three or four weeks later, the girl called and apologized for acting so foolishly. The friendship was restored.

In your job, you no doubt meet many people. Opportunities for friendships are everywhere: coworkers, families, volunteers, visitors, and your various contacts. In fact, you may be the only friend some people ever have.

So how do you make friends? Emerson said, "The only way to have a friend, is to be one." Treat others the way you would like to be treated. Hold your opinions to yourself unless asked for them. Be there when friends have a need. Weep when they weep, and rejoice when they rejoice. Concentrate on their good qualities and overlook their bad ones.

Occasionally you have tough days. That's the time to call on a friend. Remember, "When two friends share a burden, the load is only half as heavy."

Addison said, "Friendship improves happiness and abates misery by doubling our joy and dividing our grief."

And Robert Hall added, "...having a judicious and sympathetic friend also doubles our mental resources."

So why not take time today to renew an old friendship? Or how about making a new friend? You'll be glad you did. Like the old song says, "Make new friends, but keep the old, one is silver and the other gold."

CHAPTER 18

Caution: Giving Generously Can Become Habit-Forming.

Everybody likes presents. Oh, it's not necessarily the gift itself, it's the idea that someone has thought of you. But when it comes right down to it, don't you find it more meaningful to *give* a gift than to *receive* it? Think back to Christmas or Hanukkah last year. Your children or grandchildren were probably eagerly encouraging you to open your presents. But you just wanted to enjoy *their* response to the gifts you had selected for them. That is normal. Still, if you could look inside the children's hearts, you'd probably see them wanting to savor *your* delight in their gifts to you. And that is easy to understand. Giving brings pleasure.

There's a certain high that comes from giving to another. It just makes you feel good all over when you forget about yourself and give to, or do something for, someone else. And the appreciation, or even anticipated appreciation, helps create that feeling of elation. In fact, it makes you feel so good, giving can easily become a way of life.

You may give without thinking--a hug, a smile, a kind word. Maybe those things come naturally to you. You may not think of them as gifts at all. Our professions provide seemingly unlimited opportunities to give.

But what really is "giving"? It's such an overused word. Have you ever looked up *giving* in the dictionary? Webster offers numerous definitions: to transfer freely (what is one's own) to the permanent possession of another without asking anything in return; to part with, relinquish or yield; to devote one's life as to a cause; to give birth; to give one's life.

When we think of a giving person, most likely someone like Mother Theresa comes to mind. We remember her so freely and unselfishly tending the sick and dying poor in India. She, indeed, would fit the description of one who gave her life for a cause. Because of her great faith and her love of God, she gave herself totally. But, I ask you, isn't a hug to a distressed, lonely, disoriented person as great a gift? Aren't you, as the giver, equally blessing the recipient in *their* moment of need?

Many think a gift, to be worthwhile, has to be expensive, but that's not true. I remember years ago when our families were young. One sister-in-law, Keltie, had many children and lived on a shoestring, so to speak. Yet, she always gave gifts that seemed to matter. Thirty-some years later, I still have two little ceramic angels, with the month written on them in gold paint, that she gave two of my daughters at their birth. They cost about a dollar each, back then. Also, because of her thoughtfulness, our children always knew when their birthday rolled around, they would receive "mail", a personally-selected card from Aunt Keltie.

Luther said, "The heart of the giver makes the gift dear and precious." Keltie cared, and her gifts, though not costly, were indeed precious.

To further understand giving, you might compare it to gardening or farming. If you plant pepper seeds, you expect to get peppers, not radishes. If you plant tomatoes, you expect tomatoes, not broccoli. In other words, what you plant is what you will harvest. If you sow a kind word, you will most likely be answered in a kindly manner. If you are short with someone, you can expect a curt answer.

Another farming principle is that you will always reap back a much greater harvest than you plant. Let's take corn, for example. Now I'm not a farmer, so don't hold me to this, but I believe each stalk bears about two ears of corn. Once I counted the kernels on an ear, and there were almost 1000 of them. If that were seed corn, you could plant those 1000 kernels. Let's say you did, but only 500 of them actually developed. You'd still reap a harvest of half-a-million kernels. Then, if you were to plant *those* kernels, your next harvest would be 250 million kernels.

That's just like the principle of giving. You always get back *what* you sow, and you always get back *more* than you plant. If I have a financial need, I know the best thing I can do is to give to someone with a greater need. Though we don't want to give just to get something back, it always seems to work that way for me. Sometimes what we do for others seems so small, but it's so important. The benefits to you are greater than the recipient's. You know the old saying, "What goes around comes around."

I love to read about selfless people who have a love for giving. Comedian and television star, Danny Thomas, was truly a man like that. In fact, you could say he gave his life for what he believed in--St Jude's Children's Hospital. Dave Thomas, founder of the Wendy's restaurant chain, in his excellent book, *Well Done,* tells that the hospital came about as a result of a promise. In 1943, Danny was playing just five-dollar-a-week gigs, and he needed money. His wife was pregnant with their daughter, Marlo. His uncle offered him a secure job as a butcher, but Danny's heart was in being a comedian. Still, he had a wife and a coming child to support.

A devout Catholic, he stopped by a church to pray for guidance. He asked St. Jude for direction and promised to show his gratefulness if he were led correctly. Soon, he received a big-time booking at *Chef Paris* in Chicago which lasted no less than five years. This booking also launched him into his television career. Danny got so busy that he forgot his promise to show his gratitude. Upon remembering, though, after counsel from a priest, he built the best children's hospital in the world. He named it St. Jude's because that saint is given credit for impossible acts. Danny's heart and soul were in giving to, and doing for, that hospital.

Dave Thomas, goes on to tell that Danny would do fund-raising for the hospital before taking on jobs that would provide for himself. One night Danny was working late, promoting his new book so its proceeds could be forwarded to St. Jude's. Arriving home exhausted, he suffered a massive heart attack and died. But he died like he lived--giving generously of himself.

Andy Jacobs Jr. is another giver. He spent nearly 30 years as a member of the U.S. House of Representatives where he gave of himself as a public servant. Unlike many politicians, Jacobs was extremely cautious with his constituents' money. He wanted to "give back" rather than spend it on himself or needless projects. According to an Associated Press article in the *Lafayette* (Indiana) *Journal and Courier,* Jacobs had the lowest budget and the smallest staff of any member of Congress. He began refusing pay raises in 1969 because he thought they were excessive. Anything above $79,000 went back to the Treasury. Now retired from public office, he continues to give. His pension is $65,000 a year, but he plans to send part of that back. Jacobs cared about the people he represented. He personally answered every letter he received. This generous man, who served under seven presidents, thinks he may now practice law with his nephew. He admits he's apprehensive, though. According to the article, Jacobs says, "It's been a long time since I practiced law, and I don't want to charge anyone too much." He's learned the principle, "It's more blessed to give than to receive."

There are so many little ways to more greatly incorporate giving into your life. Many barely cost a thing. You might buck the popular trend and stick up for someone who is being cut down verbally. You might offer sincere compliments. You might extend a kind word to that annoying telephone solicitor before you hang up. You might hold your tongue in a meeting and let someone else have their say. You could give a flower to a coworker who is feeling down, or present another one with a big poster saying, "Thanks for all you do." You might share with others in your profession, successful ideas that have worked well for you.

Someone once said, "Presents which our love for the donor has rendered precious are ever the most acceptable."

You can also pull others up with you. Help your volunteers and assistants learn all they can, and perhaps to follow in your profession. Encourage others to push ahead. Challenge children to think broad and to dream big.

Someone I know works with a homeless mission in our town. The mission works on a "faith" budget, so to speak. But they were stretching their faith greatly trying to purchase what to them was a very expensive building, though old and needing much work. The building was desired to house a second-hand store which would be used to help residents of the mission become more self-sufficient.

When a wealthy man heard of it, he challenged them, "Why are you thinking so small?" He got them dreaming bigger and stretching their faith. Through his generous effort, he made it possible for them to get a much larger and better building. We need to dream big and chase those dreams.

Sharing our material blessings, our finances, is another great way to give. You don't have to be rich to bless others in this way. You might see a child staring longingly at the candy counter while his poor mother is counting out pennies just to buy a gallon of milk. Quietly slip the mother fifty-cents to buy a candy bar for her little one. Tipping abundantly, if you feel so led, is a great way to help struggling waiters and waitresses. And what a blessing it is to see a need, and anonymously meet it. The recipient is blessed, and you even more so. Once you've adopted the principle of giving abundantly, it will no doubt be with you for life.

I enjoy giving so much, that my husband has to keep an eye on me at conferences or he says "I'd give the store away." I love to share helpful information with my competitors. It's my belief that's there's enough to go around for everyone. But it's kind of selfish of me because when I give away, I'm the one who gets blessed.

Since giving brings such pleasure, why not let those in your care share in its rewards? Involve them in projects to bless others-- packing food baskets for the needy, crocheting slippers for the elderly, writing letters to prisoners, making crafts for a children's home.

Think again, for a moment, of the Danny Thomas hospital story. The Wendy's founder, referring to Danny's giving principles, says it better than I could: "Let a good cause, that's bigger than you, take over your life. What is your St. Jude?" he asks. "There ought to be one. Think about it and support it. Don't get scared by the word impossible. In fact, get together the best talent you can find to tackle the impossible. Do it through people. Danny got people to work together. That's the way it should be, isn't it?" he says.

I remember once, when I was an activity professional, confiding in a trusted Christian friend who happened to be a French professor at Purdue University. "Alan," I said, "I am so busy all day at the nursing home, and then at night with my family's needs, I don't have much time for ministry." Big Alan, in his soft-spoken, gentle manner just chuckled.

"Marge," he smiled knowingly, perplexed that I didn't see it. "What do you think you are doing all day at the nursing home?"

And it was like a veil was lifted from my eyes. Yes! I was giving my very best to the dear elderly in my facility whom I loved. Somehow, though, I thought since I was getting paid for doing the thing I loved so much, it didn't count in my service to God. But I learned. When you give to others, you are the one who receives the most.

So stand up professionals. Thoroughly enjoy the act of giving, and reap the fruit of your labors of love. But beware! The gift of giving can become habit-forming.

CHAPTER 19

Finding Success in Your Profession

Do you ever find yourself totally frustrated in your job? Perhaps it's one of those days when everyone is being uncooperative. Coworkers are stretching their coffee breaks to avoid work, the next shift is balking about what you didn't do, and your boss wants something done NOW!

You may feel like throwing up your hands and walking out. You may be asking if it's worth it all, or if you are spinning your wheels for nothing. You may be questioning why you even remain in this job at all. Perhaps you feel there's no chance of your being truly successful in it. But then you question, "What is success, anyway?"

Surprisingly, success is not always what you think it is. In the midst of turmoil, you may be quite successful and not even know it. If this is one of *those* days for you, believe me I understand how you feel. I, too, have experienced many of them. Even though such difficult days are few and far between, professionals can expect them to surface from time to time. The important thing is to know that, like everything else, they pass. No matter how you feel today, be assured that you are accomplishing a challenging work which many people would be unable to handle.

You are generous beyond the call of duty. You are constantly giving of your time, your talent, your love, and your energy. You are extremely patient, and you give a soft answer when you might feel like screaming. No doubt you are familiar with the saying, "You can't see the forest for the trees." Similarly, with so many responsibilities upon your shoulders, it's sometimes nearly impossible, from your point of view, to see the fruits of your labor. Consequently, you may become frustrated and question if your work is making any difference at all, or if you are really successful in what you do.

But I see your position from a different point of view. I travel and talk with people all over the country and Canada. And I hear of their frustrations. But even more, I hear of their successes. Oh, *they* may not call them successes. They see them simply as activities and daily duties. Yet, I perceive they are extremely successful. They are making life so much more meaningful for those in their care. I detect that hint of pride as they excitedly speak of their professions. And that is as it should be. You need to take pride in your work. That is part of the rewards, or the successes, of your job.

In your particular field, you must learn to measure your *own* successes and not wait for the staff to build you up. How wonderful it would be if you could count on them to give you the strokes you need. After all, it doesn't take a lot to keep professionals happy: a little recognition of your efforts, an occasional thank you, a word of appreciation, or a word of encouragement, "Keep up the good work!"

How nice it would be to occasionally hear, "I understand how you feel." or "You are so valuable to this company." or "Here, let me help!" If your staff regularly gives you the recognition you've earned, be grateful. For most of us, though, it doesn't happen. So you become responsible for finding your own rewards in your day-to-day work. Your self-esteem does not depend on others. If you use their reactions to measure your worth, you are giving them tremendous power over you. No, you learn to recognize your own worth.

So how do you perceive success? "Your answer can affect your well-being," says Frank Grazian of *Communications Briefings*. "If you see it as making lots of money, gaining recognition, or striving only for results, you may be setting yourself up for a fall," he continues. *Why?* Because you're basing your well-being on external rewards that you may be unable to control. When these fail, you suffer. Even if you gain the rewards, you might reach a point where you'll begin to question your achievements."

In your heart, you know what's really important. You don't have to look outward for strokes. Find your success in little things--a smile on a person's face, a successful community event accomplished, a met goal, knowing you are making someone's remaining time on earth more meaningful. Take pride in the work you do. Know that your work is a vital occupation. You can't be all things to all people; just be the best you can. But don't be overly concerned with results.

Expect to succeed. Dr. Wolf Rinke says, "Nothing emphasizes a positive attitude more than success. Regard success as the normal state of affairs and lack of success as the exception." Note the difference between what happens when a man says to himself, "I have failed three times and when he says "I am a failure!" My grandfather was a farmer, who with my grandmother, raised six productive children. He lived through two world wars and the Great Depression. Three times Grandpa lost everything he had. Did he stop? No! He was not a failure. He simply failed three times. Each time he pulled himself up by the boot straps and started over. When he died he left Grandma enough money to live comfortably for many years, and she even had a little left to pass on to their six children.

Don't sweat others' opinions of you or your work. Many prominent people were judged unsuccessful. Yet, sometimes success can only be seen in hindsight.

Thomas Edison was considered dumb and slow. Albert Einstein didn't walk until he was four years old. Walt Disney was fired by a newspaper for lacking ideas and went bankrupt several times before he built *Disneyland.* At Fred Astaire's first screen test, the director wrote, "can't act, slightly bald, can dance a little." Beethoven's mother called him hopeless as a composer. George Westinghouse was labeled unpractical. He was asked to leave college because his teachers determined he couldn't make it. Even so, Westinghouse secured a patent before his 20th birthday for the rotary steam engine, and his name, today, is a household word.*

We take control of our lives and build ourselves up in our struggle toward success. One way is to build yourself a success file. Maybe someone sent you a lovely note of thanks for what you did for her mom. Slip it into your file. Maybe you finally made it--you've been off smoking for a whole year. Drop a victory note in your file. Maybe your "sweetie" dropped by when you were not at your desk and left you a love note. File it. When you're having a bad day, pull out that file and smile. Know you *are* making a difference.

Linda S. Kotkin of *Kotkins Communications* recommends you start each day by asking yourself some questions: *What am I happy about in my life right now? What am I excited about in my life right now? What am I proud of in my life right now? What can I do to help someone?* These questions help you evaluate your own successes, however insignificant they may seem. Answer these questions on paper, and drop them in your success file.

Zig Ziglar, the great encourager, says, "You are not inferior or superior to anyone. You determine your success not by comparing yourself to others, rather you determine your success by comparing your accomplishments to your capabilities. You are number one when you do the best you can with what you have every day."

Success means different things to different people. Someone once said, "Success is the willingness to bear pain." Someone else said, "Success is not purchased at any one time but rather on the installment plan."

And how true those statements are! Things that come quickly and easily are seldom as appreciated as those achieved through hard work, frustration, sweat and struggle.

Will Rogers once said, "If you want to succeed in life, you've got to *know* what you are doing, *believe* in what you are doing, and *love* what you are doing. And I think that's why professionals keep at it. They know what they are doing, they believe in what they are doing, and they love what they are doing.

What I am saying is, don't be overly influenced by others' opinions of you or your position. Sure, it hurts when they don't understand your job responsibilities and think you have the "easy" job. Sure we all need stokes from others. Even so, you can survive--and even thrive--in your profession without them--if you learn to recognize your own successes and your own worth.

So give yourself and hand and take a bow. No doubt you are some of the most successful people around.

Chicken Soup for the Soul by Jack Canfield and Mark Hansen
Over the Top by Zig Ziglar

Other Books by the Author

Prices Subject to Change

How to Thrive Not Just Survive in Life and in the Activity Profession
Many books are written about residents' needs, but this one is not for them but for you, the activity professional. Designed to help you thrive in activities, it covers ways to organize your life, to make your office more manageable, to run your department on a shoestring budget, to make the phone work *for* you not against you, and how to let your excellence exceed your employer's expectations. In addition, it shows you how to handle stressful situations, to get the most out of activity conferences, and to let your activities shine out in the community. It also discusses how residents' well-being really begins with your own, how to look and feel your best, and how to dress in a professional manner. And, finally, you'll find tempting tips for your safety when you travel to activity conferences or anywhere else. Perfect-bound, 160 pages, **$21.99**.

Fun's Not Just for the Young: **"A Handbook for Recreation Leaders"**
Offers advice and ideas for those who lead activities for seniors. Covers how to make facility visits fun and easy, the benefit of humor, the history of major holidays, historical heros and heroines, presidential and First Ladies trivia, other trivia, old-time television and tricky inventions, re-living an old-fashioned Christmas, meeting residents' spiritual needs, building residents self-esteem by discovering their world, stirring up savory snacks, the mysterious magical pull of chocolate, inter-generational activities, light activities for low-functioning residents, making our melancholy men merrier, and some intriguing ideas to consider incorporating. Perfect-bound, **$21.99**.

Activities Encyclopedia: **"535 Best Activity Ideas"**
Many of these great activity ideas were contributed by activity professionals across the nation and Canada. Activities are divided into 13 categories: parties, men-only, cooking, special projects, crafts, guests, outings, games/word games, bedside and low-functioning, community outreaches, monthly biggies, and everyday activities. This user-friendly book features reinforced tabs and

alphabetized listings of activities to help you locate any activity quickly. It is also indexed. 191 pages, conveniently wiro-bound, 191 pages, **$32.99**.

Activity Planning at Your Fingertips: "All the Activities You'll Ever Need"

Activity Planning at Your Fingertips is a user-friendly guide created especially for the busy activity professional. There are over 600 activities, and two years of pre-planned activity calendars that you are free to copy and use. The book is divided into ten tabbed sections. Each section's activities are then alphabetized to help you locate any activity quickly. Formatted much like *Activities Encyclopedia,* there are activity ideas for bedside, low-functioning, holiday parties, family parties, cooking, crafts, exercise, games, fill-ins, Christmas, men-only, outings, clubs, community outreaches, special projects, monthly biggies, and everyday activities. 208 pages, wiro-bound, **$32.99**.

The Professional Activity Director: "Be All You Want to Be"

In a lively, upbeat conversational style, the author tackles such subjects as recognizing and developing your professional image, getting along with staff, dressing professionally, getting press coverage, community involvement, beating burnout, running a volunteer program, and dealing with problems common to activity directors. There are also many activity ideas, valuable resources, word games and medical terms. 174 pages, **$16.99**.

Newsletters Simplified: "Valuable Information to Print in Your Newsletter, Plus Helpful Newsletter Tips"

If you like trivia, you'll love this book. It's definitely NOT just for those who do newsletters. There are 352 pages packed full of arresting information to put in your newsletter OR to use for activities. There are reminiscent articles by Marge Knoth to copy and use. There's exciting data about Lindbergh, Earhart, Dillinger, Roosevelt, Will Rogers, Shirley Temple, and more. In addition, you'll find facts about the 1920's, 30's, 40's, World War I and II, and the Great Depression. You'll also find presidential trivia, holiday trivia, quotable quotes, old-time prices, one-liners, comforting scriptures, and funny stories told by nursing home residents. There are also five "how-to" chapters to help you put together a great newsletter. Perfect-bound, 352 pages, **$22.99**.

Remembering the Good Old Days: **"Lively Reminiscent Group Starters"**
This book is all you need to lead a lively reminiscence group with no prior planning. Offers 100 old-time subjects, each broken down into thoughtful questions (which lead to the answers) which quickly draw the elderly into discussion. Some subjects are: old-time beauty secrets, barn dances, immigration, dance marathons, famous people, preserving food, weddings, and childbirth. There are 21 tips for leading a lively reminiscence group, photos and illustrations, old-time prices, and 19th-century helpful hints. Perfect-bound, 130 pages, **$14.99**.

Looking Back: **"Reminiscent Party Fun for Senior Citizens--200 Questions and Answers"**
Offers 200 challenging questions and answers about life long ago. Also one-liner "Do You Remember?" discussion starters. Great for any time you need a quick activity or want to stimulate the elderly to reminisce. Lots of photos and illustrations. Perfect-bound, 85 pages, **$11.99**.

Marge Knoth